# ART-SONG IN AMERICA

A STUDY
IN THE DEVELOPMENT OF
AMERICAN MUSIC

*By*

WILLIAM TREAT UPTON

$3.00

Boston : OLIVER DITSON COMPANY : New York

Chicago: LYON & HEALY, Inc.          London: WINTHROP ROGERS, Ltd.

MADE IN U. S. A.

TO MY WIFE

# PREFACE

THIS volume lays no claim to being an encyclopedic history of Art-song in America. It presents no report of any committee of experts, no findings of any learned commission. It is simply and solely the result of devoted and enthusiastic study on the part of one individual. Whatever of value it may possess is due to the fact that it is a genuine study of American song itself rather than study about American song. Whether it be a loss or a gain that this study has been so purely individual on the part of the author is, of course, a debatable question—one may only express the possible hope that what it lacks in accumulated authority it may perhaps gain in unity of viewpoint.

At any rate it is primarily a study in the development of one particular phase of American music and only secondarily a history of this same phase. Nothing more than a skeletonized historical background has been sought for, merely enough to identify to a certain extent the earlier songs and their writers. Even this has been entirely discarded in the later chapters.

If it shall seem that certain songs and certain song-writers have been omitted that should have been included (and such is absolutely certain to be the case), the author craves pardon in advance for such unintended omissions and wishes to remind the reader that complete comprehensiveness in so large a field is scarcely to be expected of one fallible mind.

He feels himself under the deepest obligations to Carl Engel, Walter R. Whittlesey, and the other members of the staff of the Music Division of the Library of Congress for their unfailing courtesy and assistance in making the researches in that remarkable collection a memorable and delightful experience; to William

Arms Fisher for his interest from the first inception of the work; and, one might almost say, most of all to those invaluable pioneer researches in the field of early American music by Oscar G. Sonneck, without which all our present-day efforts would seem almost hopeless.

He wishes also to express his gratitude to *The Musical Quarterly* and *The Musical Observer* for permission to include in this book certain portions which had earlier appeared in their columns; and to express to the following publishing houses his deep appreciation of their kindness in permitting such generous quotation from their copyright songs: G. Schirmer, Inc., New York; Oliver Ditson Company, Boston; Arthur P. Schmidt Company, Boston; Boston Music Company, Boston; Composers' Music Corporation, New York; Carl Fischer, Inc., New York; J. Fischer and Bro., New York; Associated Music Publishers, New York; H. W. Gray Company, New York; G. Ricordi and Company, New York; Theo. Presser Company, Philadelphia; John Church Company, Cincinnati.

*William Treat Upton*

Oberlin, Ohio, June 8, 1930.

# CONTENTS

IX

# CONTENTS

# CHAPTER I

## 1750-1800

*Francis Hopkinson, James Bremner, William Selby,*

*P. A. von Hagen*

JUST as it has sometimes seemed that the best pumpkin pie has the least pumpkin in it, so it may very well be that in any introduction to the subject of early American song similar proportions should hold with regard to early American song itself! For whatever else our early forefathers may have done with success, not much can be said for their songs. And if we tentatively but laboriously define art-song to be that particular species of the general song-form which is used for the conscious solution of some musico-aesthetic problem imposed by its text, then very little evidence of true art-song is to be found in the days of our early American song writers. And yet, fortunately, there is even in these earlier beginnings just enough suggestion of the art-song of the future to establish a logical connection and to give hints, vague though they be, of that which is to come.

It is for us of today a far leap into the past to call to mind Francis Hopkinson, the contemporary and friend of George Washington; yet it seems reasonable to consider that our song began with him. Who, then, was Francis Hopkinson, and how was he the pioneer in American song?

A lifelong citizen of Philadelphia, Francis Hopkinson (1737-1791) was born when that city, foremost of American cities in many respects, was lamentably behind in musical affairs. In his young manhood, however, he saw the beginning of that steady musical progress which at just about the time of his death

1

was to reach what has been called Philadelphia's "golden age"— the years 1790 to 1850. In this progress he undoubtedly had no small share. We know that he was a skilful performer on both the harpsichord and organ, that he trained choral bodies in church singing, that he wrote church music, and what is most interesting to us, the fact seems to be established that he was "our first poet-composer in general and of songs in particular" (Sonneck). He was well trained in music, possessed an excellent musical library (rather Italian in its tendencies), was apparently well-read musically—in short, he was a cultured musical amateur. A lawyer by profession, a graduate of the College of Philadelphia in 1757, A.M., 1760, LL.D., 1790, also A.M. (hon.), College of New Jersey, 1763. He was also a signer of the Declaration of Independence and held important offices under the new Republic. We can readily understand that through his personal prestige he was able to accomplish much for the cause of music. It was probably in 1759 that he wrote his first song, *My Days have been so wondrous Free*, the song that we always associate with his name and which we may well consider as the beginning of that long line of American songs which forms the subject of our present study. In the style of the time it is written in but two parts, treble and bass, the filling in of the harmony being left to the accompanist, or played simply as it stands. While no one would call it in any sense a great song, it has its own merits, and although chiefly interesting from its historical importance, it is not entirely without value from a purely musical standpoint. Hopkinson seems to have had an excellent melodic gift; his little tunes move along in a manner not undistinguished. One never feels that they are commonplace. In this song there is a frequent recurrence of a repeated passing-note in the melody, a distinctly instrumental effect which when given to the voice almost approximates a syncopation. Harmonically there is little of interest and it has to be admitted that the tiny postlude seems to be characterized by what the rest of the song so happily lacks—complete mediocrity.

Another song, *Rondo* from *Seven Songs,* published in 1788 and dedicated to George Washington, shows faint foreshadowings of real art-song technique. The deft treatment of the words "This whining and pining" is anything but perfunctory, the bit of imitative work at "Curse my fortune" is delightfully sophisti-

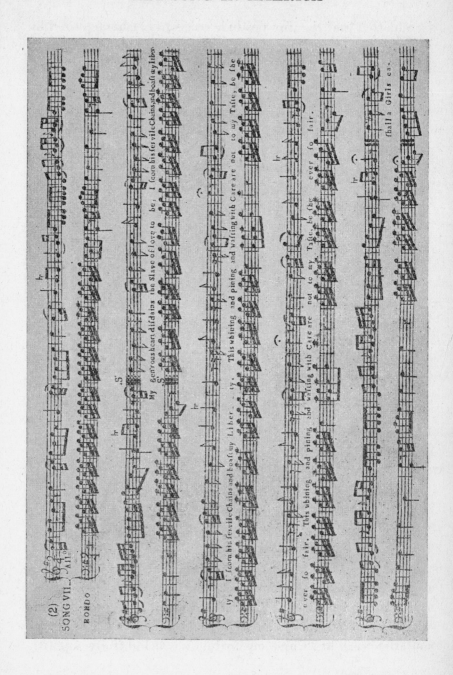

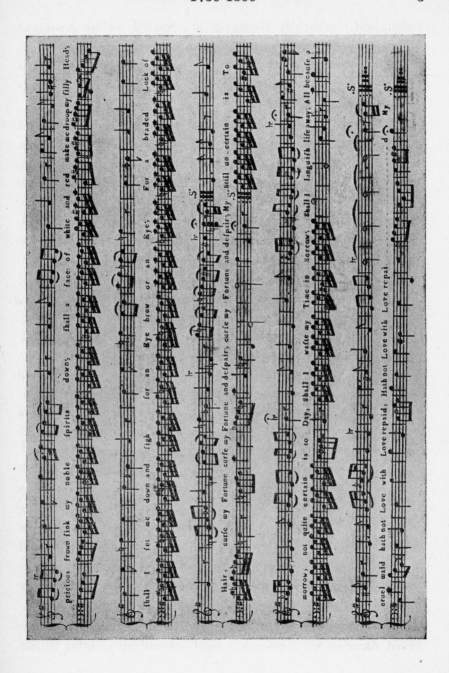

cated, and the turn to the minor at "Shall I set me down and sigh" is as psychologically correct in the eighteenth century as in the twentieth. So that musically as well as historically it is entirely fitting that we begin our studies with these early songs of Francis Hopkinson.

If we observe the musical background against which we must project this figure of our first secular song-writer, in the years, let us say, 1750 to 1800, we find it purely English, with no slightest sign of that all-pervasive German influence which is to come later. It seems clear that from about 1730 until well into the nineteenth century this English influence was predominant. The question then naturally arises as to what England was doing in music at this time and how it was to influence America.

In England it was the time of those writers and compilers of ballad opera—Arne, Linley, Arnold, Dibdin, Shield, Storace and others, who, basing their work upon the extraordinarily successful *Beggar's Opera* (1732), had evolved a type of ballad-opera peculiarly their own, related of course to the folk-operas of other countries in that it also consisted of plays interspersed with music, but still possessing a very real individuality. To be sure these operas often deteriorated into mere *pasticcio* form, a hodge-podge of melodies gathered at random from any source whatsoever; but at their best estate they were works of both virility and grace. It behooves us to look upon these men with respect and admiration for the very real ability shown in many of these operas. To one who leafs through these fascinating old scores in the Library of the British Museum there comes the realization that this first definite and powerful influence brought to bear upon our early American music was decidedly wholesome; a fact often overlooked in the time of our later, more zealous devotion to all that was German in music.

With the question as to how this music reached and influenced America we approach a most interesting chapter in our musical relations with England both before and after the Revolutionary war, for it seems that England continually sent of her very best to entertain and educate this rather independent daughter of hers in the West.

It was in 1750 that we in America had our first taste of the *Beggar's Opera*, and from that time on ballad operas came in a copious stream from England.   In the last fifteen years of the century something like fifty different operas by the English composers already mentioned were produced, as well as a few by Rousseau and Grétry in English form, some of these quickly passing out of sight, others holding their own for a long season, quite as is the wont of opera today.   We are not as familiar with the musical interpreters of these early works as we are of the later, but we know of the presence in America as early as 1766 of Miss Wainwright and Stephen Wools, both capable English singers, and reputed to have had the distinction of being pupils of Dr. Arne.   As we approach the new century we find the list of singers constantly growing in interest and importance.

The *Euterpiad* (New York, April 15, 1830), quoting from some London magazine in regard to the status of music in America past and present, refers to Incledon and Phillips as the first English vocalists to visit New York, and states that the latter gave the greater satisfaction, his singing of Moore's melodies being particularly pleasing.   In this connection we may note that the first song in the earliest volume of old copyright songs in the Library of Congress at Washington—that priceless collection of early American music—is the following song by this same Philipps: *"The Hunter's Horn,* a new sporting Cavatina sung by Mr. Philipps with the most unbounded applause at the vocal concerts, Dublin, at the Theatre Royal, Crow St., and at the New York Theatre.   Composed by T. Phillips.   Copyright secured, New York.   Published for the composer by Geib and Co., 23 Maiden Lane."   It is marked as received at the

Department of State May 28, 1819, by Daniel Brent, Chief Clerk. Phillips' colleague, Incledon, it seems, was successful with the rough sea songs, but pelted off the stage in *Beggar's Opera!*

The article quoted above adds that Mrs. Knight (formerly Miss Povey) of Drury Lane was "the first English lady of talent to visit America," and that she, too, was more successful in ballads than in opera. She was closely followed by Miss George of the Haymarket Theatre and Drury Lane, and with her begins the really brilliant succession of young artists coming to us from London. Miss George was not restricted in her abilities to ballads, as her predecessors had been, but was equally at home in opera and oratorio, with a voice of great compass, and the reputation, as a singer, of being quite unsurpassed on the English stage for taste and skill in vocal technique. Later, as Mrs. Oldmixon, she continued to hold a secure place in the admiration of American audiences for many years. Among others well known in England who came to America at this time and were to make the early years of the nineteenth century notable in operatic annals were Miss Broadhurst from Covent Garden, not yet twenty years old; the Darleys, who possessed an excellent reputation in England; John Hodgkinson, real name Meadowcraft, twenty-six years old, versatile and brilliant, who had won his spurs at Bath and was just about to begin his London career, a tragedian, comedian and richly endowed singer, called in England "the provincial Garrick"; Miss Brett, afterward his wife; Mrs. Pownall, who as Mrs. Wrighten had achieved a distinguished success at Drury Lane, notable for her skill both as singer and actress and beloved for the sincerity and generosity of her character. So it will be seen that even in these early days audiences in Philadelphia and New York and later in Boston were treated to no second-rate performances.

That the works performed were, according to the standards

of the day, worthy of the eminent singers and comparable to, and in general identical with those given in London is shown by Mr. Sonneck's study of this question in his *Early Opera in America*.  Not only were the same works given in America to a great extent, but they even suffered no great delay in their overseas production, the American *première* often following more closely upon that in England than we would have expected. Our forefathers seem already to have had the true American fondness for being up to date in all things, musical as well as otherwise.  It would seem to be typical that one of the earliest performances of Handel's *Messiah* (if indeed not the very earliest) to be given outside of England was that in America in 1770.  We must promptly disabuse our minds of any idea that America was nothing but a crude, raw country, destitute of any culture.  Crude and raw in many respects it must have been, but there were true music lovers then as now, and we were not so far behind the rest of the world as we sometimes think.  Rather we were a true child of English culture and one of whom she needed not to be ashamed.

In a material way, too, we were ambitious, as is shown by the fact that we provided adequate and dignified edifices for the accommodation of these operatic entertainments.  The article in the *Euterpiad*, quoted above, continues, "The Park Theatre . . . . affords means of giving more effect to dramatic productions of every description than any theatre in England—the metropolis excepted"; and we read elsewhere that the New Theatre, Philadelphia (1793-94), was considered one of the seven wonders of America; as large as Covent Garden, and an exact copy of the Theatre Royal at Bath, England.

It is interesting, also, to learn that during these years orchestral music was flourishing, and though performed by smaller and less efficient orchestras, much of the best orchestral music of Europe was being heard here.  So that to such men as Francis

Hopkinson and other ardent amateurs in the art of music there were even here in America opportunities for culture not at all to be despised.

At this time, too, began that migration to America of musicians from other lands which a little later was to mean so much to our musical development. James Bremner, organist, composer, and probably Hopkinson's teacher, a relative of Robert Bremner, well known English music publisher, came to Philadelphia in 1763, and died there in 1780. William Selby, born in England 1738, came to America about 1770 and from that time until his death in Boston in 1798 was one of the central figures in the musical life of that city. He was organist, harpsichordist, teacher, concert promoter; wrote a concerto for harpsichord, a quartet sonata, organ pieces, anthems, and songs. But so far as is known, none of these has been preserved. Peter Albrecht von Hagen came to America 1774, originally from Rotterdam, but more lately from London. He was a pupil of Honauer in Paris and son of P. A. von Hagen, organist and violinist in Rotterdam. After spending some time in Charleston he came to New York in 1789, and to Boston 1796. He died in 1803.

It is in this same period (1750-1800) that we see the disrupting effect of the war of the Revolution, in the course of which music naturally came to a standstill; and at its conclusion the comfortable and easy-going status of colonial life was exchanged for the uncertainties and responsibilities of a new and untried State, slowly and tentatively developing its own political and art consciousness, all of which we find reflected in its music.

From our point of view, then, we may perhaps consider it as the time when the stage was being set for the appearance of American song as such; that its only representative along the direct line of our study is in the person of Francis Hopkinson, who is a figure, as I have tried to show, of no little importance in the beginning of the study of our subject.

# CHAPTER II

## 1800-1825

*Alexander Reinagle, Raynor Taylor, Benjamin Carr,*

*James Hewitt, Victor Pelissier, Gottlieb Graupner*

A T the beginning, then, of the nineteenth century, we find in America many excellent singers engaged for the most part in giving performances of ballad operas, together with numerous more or less capable orchestral groups; but what is more to our purpose, we find in the last decade of the passing century a pronounced increase in that influx of musicians from Europe, who by their skill and musicianship, their wide knowledge of musical affairs in England and on the Continent were to prove so helpful in this crucial time. Alexander Reinagle, Raynor Taylor, and Benjamin Carr in Philadelphia; James Hewitt and Victor Pelissier in New York; Gottlieb Graupner in Boston—all these are names that we Americans do well to honor; for these men came to America, made their permanent homes here and deliberately took upon themselves the task of seeing to it that America should hear the best music of the world so far as it was possible to do so; and through their arrangements and at times necessary simplifications of the works of the European masters, and their own original compositions, they laid the foundations upon which we have been building ever since. Fortunately we are still in possession of some of these arrangements and original compositions in the Library of Congress.

Of these men the first to reach America was Alexander Reinagle, of Austrian descent but born in England in 1756, who reached New York in 1786 but left shortly afterwards for Philadelphia where he resided permanently; died in Baltimore, 1809. Reinagle was pianist, composer, and manager of theatrical enterprises, a musician of high ideals and capabilities, so much so in fact that he was highly esteemed by Carl Philipp Emanuel

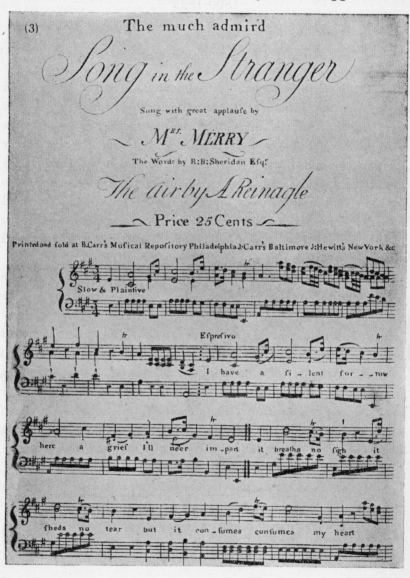

**2**

This cherish'd woe this lov'd despair
My lot for ever be
So my souls lord the pangs to bear
Be never known by thee

**3**

And when pale characters of death
Shall mark this alter'd cheek
When my poor wasted trembling breath
My lifes last hope shall seek

**4**

I shall not raise my eyes to heav'n
Nor mercy ask for me
My soul despairs to be forgiv'n
Unpardon'd love by thee

FLUTE

GUITTAR

Secur'd according to Law

Bach who is said to have asked for his silhouette that it might be included in his collection of those of his friends and the celebrities of the day. Reinagle's teacher in Scotland had been Raynor Taylor who was soon to follow him to America. Reinagle's songs at their best show abounding vigor, firm texture—due primarily to his use of dissonance—and a melody that is broad and dignified. His initial themes are flexible, often extending throughout the compass of an octave. His harmonic style is less free than that of his teacher Raynor Taylor. This conservatism is shown, for instance, in the fact that his dissonances, when used at all, are carefully prepared. His song *I have a Silent Sorrow* (R. B. Sheridan) is really an excellent little song.

Raynor Taylor, who followed Reinagle to Philadelphia in 1793, was born in England probably in 1747, and died in Philadelphia in 1825. He was organist, pianist, famous for his powers of improvisation, and had been a recognized composer of ballads in England before coming to America. In his songs he was much given to following a very fixed structural program, generally modulating both toward the dominant and relative minor in the course of the same song, rarely toward the subdominant. Most of these songs were short and of the simplest construction. Harmonically he was very free for his time, making frequent use of unprepared dissonance and even at times introducing the chord on the second degree—none too grammatically, it is to be feared. In *Jockey and Jenny* he employs imitation between the voice part and the bass of the accompaniment, and in a *Rondo* for piano makes effective use of true canon. Apparently Taylor was a musician not afraid to go his own way!

Last, but probably most important of our Philadelphia group is Benjamin Carr who also arrived in 1793. He was born in England about 1769, and died in Philadelphia in 1831.

Younger than either of his colleagues, he outlived them both by several years. He was a leader in every worth-while musical movement in Philadelphia, a man of large and wholesome influence. That the city of his adoption was not unappreciative

(4) JOCKEY AND JENNY

Composed by
R. Taylor

PHILADELPHIA. Printed for the Author Nº. 96 North sixth street; And sold by B. Carr at his Musical repository Market St. And by I. Carr Baltimore. Price ¼ of a Dollar

Allegretto

Near a shady Myrtle Bow'r JOCKEY once was straying  JENNY chanc'd to

pass that way JENNY had been maying  a maying  a May..ing

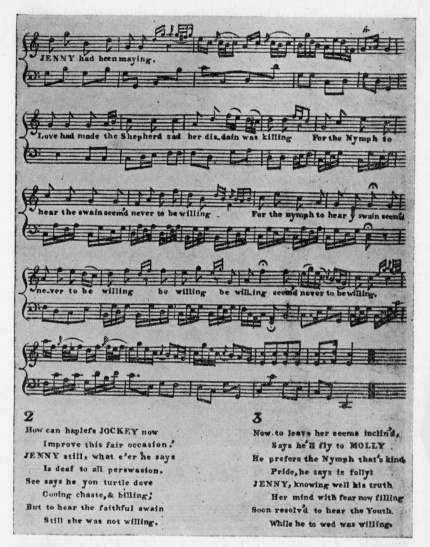

JENNY had been maying.

Love had made the Shepherd sad her dis_dain was killing    For the Nymph to

hear the swain seem'd never to be willing    For the nymph to hear y swain seem'd

ne_ver to be willing    be willing    be will_ing    seem'd never to be willing.

**2**
How can hapless JOCKEY now
  Improve this fair occasion?
JENNY still, what e'er he says
  Is deaf to all perswasion.
See says he yon turtle dove
  Cooing chaste, & billing;
But to hear the faithful swain
  Still she was not willing.

**3**
Now to leave her seems inclin'd,
  Says he'll fly to MOLLY
He prefers the Nymph that's kind,
  Pride, he says is folly;
JENNY, knowing well his truth,
  Her mind with fear now filling
Soon resolv'd to hear the Youth.
  While he to wed was willing.

is shown in the fact that at his death a monument was erected to
his memory. One of his songs, *Ah! how Hapless is the Maiden*,
was sung by the most distinguished singers of his day—Mrs.
Oldmixon, Mrs. Hodgkinson, and Miss Broadhurst. It is a
coloratura song abounding in scales and sequences of broken

thirds, stiff and utterly lacking in spontaneity. This florid type
was apparently not congenial to Carr, for the more lyric portions come off better, being dignified and worthy. His opera,
*The Archers*, performed in 1796, has sometimes been called the
first American opera, but it now seems that this honor must go

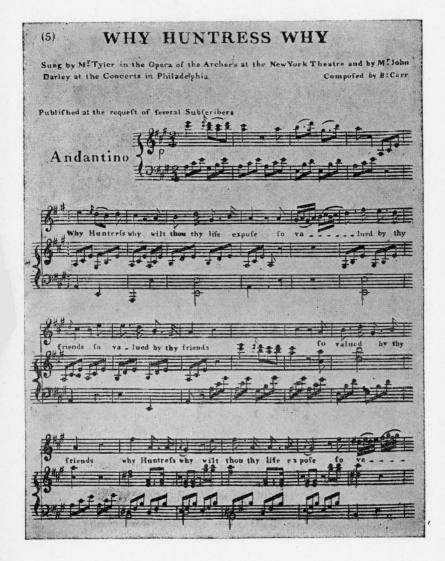

Ah! think what pangs thy Father still must feel
What pangs must Arnold know
When thou'rt expos'd unto the biting steel
Shall rush amid the foe
Then huntress why &c

elsewhere. We have remaining from this opera a *Rondo* from the overture, arranged for piano, and the air *Why, Huntress, Why?* This latter is attractive, and interesting for its rhythmic combinations, the voice almost constantly taking ♪. ♪ against a triplet of eighth notes in the accompaniment. When, however, the voice takes ♫♫ the accompanying triplet drops out, thus avoiding the conflict of four against three! Carr sometimes made use of augmented harmonies. Without question his most successful song is *Hymn to the Virgin—Ave Maria—*Number Three of "Six Ballads from the poem *The Lady of the Lake*" (Scott), Op. VII, published in 1810 by Carr and Schetky, Philadelphia, a splendidly preserved copy of which is in the Library of Congress. This *Ave Maria* is really a remarkable song for its time, and I hazard the claim that its principal theme

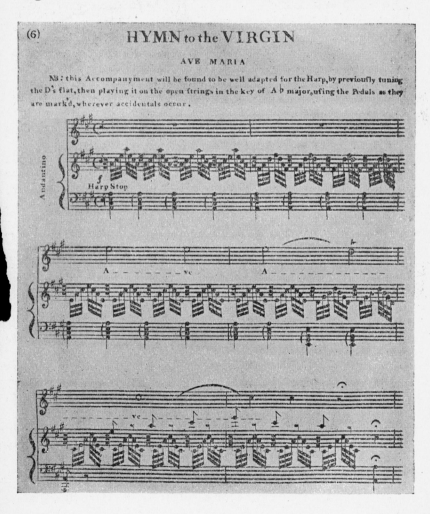

(fourth score) is the most touchingly beautiful phrase in all early
American song.   Here begins art in song—conscious, beautiful
art.

This use of a long sustained tone, flowering out at its close
into the most delicate shades and tints, is characteristic of Carr
and here shows at its very best.   There is at the Library of the
British Museum a most interesting composition of Mr. Carr's,
published in London, unfortunately without date, entitled "*Poor
Richard*, a favorite Ballad, words by Mr. John Carr, composed
by B. Carr, and sung in the Principal Concerts of England . .
London, Printed and Sold by J. Bland, at his Music Ware-
house; No. 45, Holborn."   This is elaborately orchestrated for

2 horns, 2 flutes, 2 violins, 2 bassoons, cembalo, viola and bass.
The orchestration is not unskilfully done, and the interludes
contain effective part-writing for the various instruments.

The two outstanding musicians at this same early period in
New York, James Hewitt and Victor Pelissier, both arrived
there at the same time that Raynor Taylor and Benjamin Carr
came to Philadelphia, in those years so notable for the various
beginnings of serious musical adventure in America—1792,
1793. Hewitt, violinist, composer and publisher, was born in
England, 1770; died at New York, 1827. He seems to have
been to New York what Carr was to Philadelphia, the leading
spirit in all musical affairs. He came to New York in company
with several others, Bergman, Young, Phillips, and Jean Gehot,
all "professors of music from the opera house, Hanover Square,
and Professional Concerts under the direction of Haydn, Pleyel,
etc., London" (it will be noted that in those days the term "pro-
fessor" seems to have indicated professional musician as contrasted with amateur). The other members of this group were
helpful in raising the standard of orchestral playing in America
but left no particular record as composers, although Gehot is
known to have written quartets, trios, etc., all trace of which has
been lost. In furnishing a musical background for the declamation of Collins' *Ode on the Passions* in 1795, Hewitt seems to
have been the first in America to write melodrama. He also
wrote the opera *Tammany* (1794) and various musical numbers
for *The Patriot* (1794), *Columbus* (1797), and other similar
works. His song *In a far distant clime I have left a sweet rose*
(180 -) is charmingly simple and Mozartian. He was subject,
however, to the same modulatory timidity that we observed in the
case of the Philadelphia writers, although his song *In vain the
tears of anguish flow* (180 -) is unusually elaborate for him,
having beside the customary turn toward the dominant in the
first part, a second section in the parallel minor which touches its
own relative major before returning to the original first section.

Quite a little journey into the world!

Hewitt's colleague in New York, Victor Pelissier, is notable for having written the first American opera, *Edwin and Angelina* (text based on Goldsmith), produced in 1794, thus antedating Carr's *Archers* by two years. His songs are very

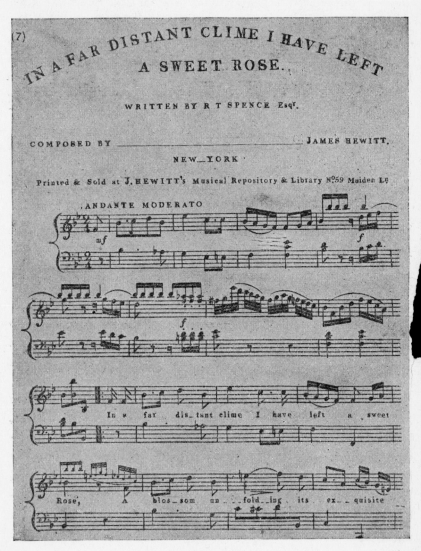

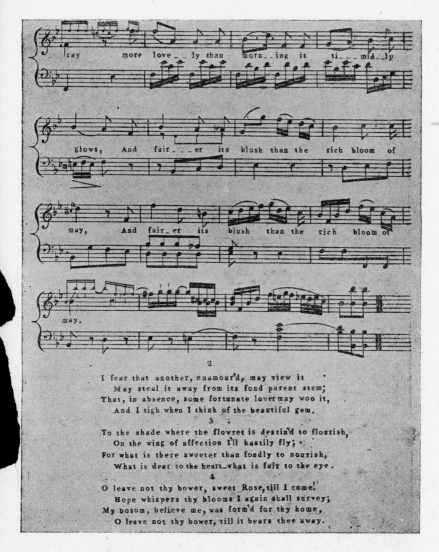

I fear that another, enamour'd, may view it
  May steal it away from its fond parent stem;
That, in absence, some fortunate lover may woo it,
  And I sigh when I think of the beautiful gem.
        3
To the shade where the flowret is destin'd to flourish,
  On the wing of affection I'll hastily fly;
For what is there sweeter than fondly to nourish,
  What is dear to the heart—what is fair to the eye.
        4
O leave not thy bower, sweet Rose, till I come!
  Hope whispers thy blooms I again shall survey;
My bosom, believe me, was form'd for thy home,
  O leave not thy bower, till it bears thee away.

smooth, flowing and lyric but seem to show less vigor, less dissonant character than those of Taylor.  He developed the accompaniment into an independent part, with a separate staff for
the voice.  Like others of his time he was much given to having
the voice sustain one tone through two or three measures while

the accompaniment took the melody—an effect much beloved by Shield, Storace and all their school.

Last of all comes Boston with Gottlieb Graupner, born in Germany 1767, who after spending a couple of years in Charles-

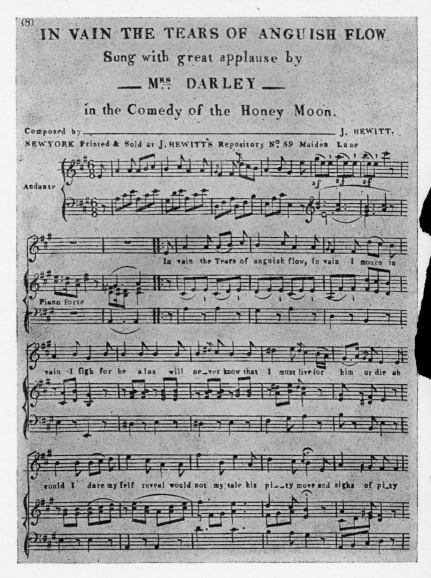

ton reached Boston in 1797 and was for many years her sole and final arbiter in all things musical, and remained her most prominent musician until his death in 1836. And, let it be noted, here for the first time Germany enters upon the scene. England is still predominant, but with Pelissier there comes a touch of French, with Graupner of German, although undoubtedly influenced and modified by his seven years stay in London, for he had also been playing in orchestral performances there under Haydn, having been oboist in a Hanoverian regiment before leaving home. What a Mecca to musicians from all lands was London in those days! Like many another coming to us from foreign countries, Graupner seems at once to have become interested in the possibilities of negro song, and as early as 1799, at the end of the second act of *Oroonoko* in the Federal Street Theatre, he interpolated the song *The Gay Negro Boy*, given in costume and with banjo accompaniment. It is much to be doubted that this was an authentic negro melody; it was far more likely nothing but the ancient progenitor of those quasi-negro tunes with which the numerous minstrel troupes were to flood the country a few decades later. A better tribute to his musical worth and capabilities is that he should be called "the father of American orchestral music," from the fact that he gathered together the group of orchestral players who probably formed the nucleus of Boston's Philharmonic Orchestra which lasted for some fifteen years, a record for those times.

# CHAPTER III

## 1825-1850

*George J. Webb, Charles E. Horn, Henry C. Watson,*

*F. N. Crouch, William R. Bristow, Henry Russell,*

*J. P. Knight, J. L. Hatton, Anton Philipp Heinrich*

*("Father" Heinrich), George P. H. Loder, Elam Ives, Jr.,*

*William A. King, Charles Jarvis, James Flint,*

*George Henry Curtis*

WE have seen that since the Revolution, as before it, English musicians continued to come to us, and we know something of their ideals and of their work in our midst. But of just what constituted the underlying popular consciousness, its uncertainty and confusion of thought, its recklessness and roughness of conduct such as always follow in the wake of war, of all this it is difficult to draw a definite picture. And yet it is seen in the music of the time. For this reason these years form what is in many respects one of the most interesting, if at the same time most crude, of all the earlier periods of our musical development. For this flood of commonplaceness flowed on in ever-increasing volume until it would seem that the possibilities of mediocrity were well nigh exhausted. One who goes through the files of the copyright songs of this period in the Library of Congress must stand appalled at the tawdriness of the musical output. Ballads of course predominated—sentimental, comic, descriptive, Ethiopian ("nigger" songs), political campaign songs, ad infinitum! The worst offenders in bringing all this vulgarity before the public were undoubtedly the various "fam-

29

ilies"—the Hutchinsons, the Rainer, Barker, Houser, Bohannan and other families, the different miscellaneous groups such as the Alleghanians and the Moravians, and the numerous minstrel clubs.   And yet after all we must not be too harsh in our judgments on these early efforts.   There were glimpses of serious intent even here.   It was not all coarse and vulgar or of a sickly sentimentality.   There must have been some rather attractive singing by various and sundry of these organizations, and even the work of the minstrels themselves bore rich fruit in the songs of Stephen C. Foster.   All this type of musical expression belonged solely to the people—it was racy of the soil, of every-day life and experience.   Neither *"Mr. and Mrs. Jones' Discussion on Dress,* a comic Matrimonial Duett," nor *Old Arm Chair* would quite reflect the popular fancy of the twentieth century, nor the various songs "sung by Ossian Dodge at his fashionable entertainments throughout the Union" which came a little later, but they were probably true to the taste of their day.   Along with these were the numerous and elaborate Odes, for the most part long and empty, but sometimes showing a real feeling for the dignity of their subjects, as in the case of Charles Edward Horn's *Ode to Washington* and George H. Curtis' Scena Religiosa *Absalom.*

Of those first missioners on our musical frontiers, mentioned above, Bremner, Selby, Reinagle and von Hagen have died, but others have come in their places.   From England, George J. Webb in 1830, Charles E. Horn 1833, B. E. Woolf 1839, Henry C. Watson 1840, Richard Hoffmann 1847, F. N. Crouch 1849. Horn, composer of *Cherry Ripe* and *I've been roaming,* and Crouch, the talented but erratic composer of *Kathleen Mavourneen,* came as mature men in their forties, Watson, writer and critic, at thirty-five, Webb in his twenties, Hoffmann at seventeen, Woolf a mere infant.   Each played his part, whether greater or less, in our musical upbuilding.

We should also note that there had come from England in 1824 a young man of twenty-one years, William R. Bristow, organist, teacher, conductor, who in 1840 was organist at St. Patrick's Cathedral, New York, and publishing some excellent church music. His chief interest to us, however, lies in the fact that he was the father of George F. Bristow, of whom we are to hear much presently. In the thirties came Henry Russell, prolific writer of ballads, sea-songs and all sorts of descriptive songs of most vivid type, who spent some eight years here; and J. P. Knight made us a visit of two years (1839-1841) leaving as his memorial that song still so dear to the heart of every basso-profundo, *Rocked in the Cradle of the Deep* (1840). J. L. Hatton (1848) also is remembered for his song *The Protestant*.

But perhaps the most important event of this period is the distinct and definite entrance of Germany into the musical life of America. Otto Dresel, who first came to New York in 1848, at the age of twenty-two, as concert pianist and teacher, and after a brief visit in Germany made his permanent home in Boston where he died in 1890, was without doubt the most thoroughly equipped musician who had as yet come to America, and his influence was as admirable as it was far-reaching. Wulf Fries, the 'cellist, twenty-two years old, had come in 1847, and the fourteen-year-old Frederic Brandeis from Austria followed in 1849, the former settling in Boston (died 1902), the latter in New York (died 1899). Building upon the foundations already laid by Graupner, these men helped to rear in the new world the stately and enduring edifice of German supremacy in musical art.

In some ways even more vital to our particular study, however, is the existence at this time of a group of young musicians, actually born in America and in that sense the first *bona fide* American musicians with whom we have come in contact, whose work now begins to come into view, available for study. But since their more representative and mature efforts do not appear until later, we will content ourselves for the present with the mere mention of their names: Wm. H. Fry, 1813-1864; Francis Boott, 1813-1904; J. M. Deems, 1818-1901; Richard Storrs Willis, 1819-1900; George F. Bristow, 1825-1898; Stephen C. Foster, 1826-1864; Lucien H. Southard, 1827-1881.

We spoke a moment ago of the decisive entry of Germany into our midst. But hers was not the only foreign influence during this period. When English tradition and prestige ultimately gave way before the advance of Germany, it was but the final and happy outcome of many interesting skirmishes between various foreign musical influences, each trying to establish itself on American soil. From 1825 to 1832 something of Italian opera had been heard (mostly Rossini), and at times American interest seemed fairly divided between the English ballad operas and the French operas of Boieldieu and others. But in 1832 through the efforts of the well-known Italian librettist, Lorenzo da Ponte, then living in America and who wished to give America a chance to hear the best Italian operas worthily presented, a complete Italian opera company was brought to America with the result that there ensued a lively war between its partisans and those of the English ballad-operas. The Italians created great interest as can be seen from the many American reprints of Italian operatic airs during these years. There is no doubt that Italian fluency and lyricism had great influence and made themselves very much felt for a time; but owing to the excellence of the English singers then in America and the traditional fondness of the American public for the English ballad-opera, the latter finally won out. That it should in its turn yield to the higher influence of the German type of music was inevitable. It was interesting and of value, however, that our early music should have added something of Italian grace, of French finesse, to its sturdy English foundation before coming completely under that dominant German influence which in itself was one of the most striking phenomena of the nineteenth century.

It is always interesting to get contemporary views of events that have passed into history, and we find an illuminating sidelight upon these English-Italian cross-currents in the following excerpt from our earliest musical publication, the Boston *Euterpeiad*, in its issue for December 30, 1820: "The English expect that sense is to hold equal if not superior reign with sound. They demand, particularly, a bold, plain, nervous elocution, freed alike from timid and from weak expression. They regard pure tone and articulation more than flowing execution. They ask a few graces, but these neither commonplace nor of vulgar structure. They wish to have their higher affections rather than their lower appetites moved and excited. Such are the attributes of the English school, properly so called . . . . English style, properly so called, is conversant with none of the modern arts of voluptuous insinuation. Purcell, Handel, Arne, Jackson and Crotch are the most genuine English composers we have . . . . Their music produces none of the effects of Italian seduction. It is purely intellectual and adapted to manly sentiment. Many contemporaries, Mr. Webbe, Dr. Callcott, Mr. Horsley and Mr. Attwood are of a sterling metal. Whilst most popular ballads . . . . are a mongrel breed, possessing neither the grace of their Italian, nor the strength of their English parents."

And while we are in this reminiscent mood, let us make one further quotation, this time a letter, apparently from England, appearing in the *Euterpiad* (New York) for July 15, 1830: "What has become of our good old songs, which used to draw tears from every eye and inspire a kindred feeling in every breast? Who now will presume to ask for the fine heart-thrilling airs of the last century? What Miss at her piano or harp has ever heard of Handel's songs, or can play you a delicate

morceau of Haydn, or a touching aria of the enchanting
Mozart?   Instead of these treasures, these gems from the deep
mine of the heart, she will rattle you off *I'd be a Butterfly,
Love's Ritornella, Love was once a little Boy,* and a whole
rackload of Bayley's, Barnett's and Parry's vapid, childish,
nonsensical stuff."   With due allowance for time, place, and
circumstance, hasn't this a strangely familiar sound?

These years are made notable, as far as American publication goes, by the first appearance in America of any song by
Schubert issued by an American press.   In 1847, published by
Ferrett, Philadelphia, we find *La Fille du Pecheur,* with English
words, adapted from the French!   Surely a circuitous route for
a simple Schubert song!   In 1848, *Die Forelle* appears as *The
Child, the Butterfly and the Rose,* again from the French.
Franz Abt also makes his American debut with *When the Swal-
lows homeward Fly.*

Before leaving this period, a national, almost international
figure must be presented here.   One hesitates to enter upon a
discussion of this unique character, for a volume could scarcely
do him justice, to say nothing of a paragraph!   To anyone
studying these particular years a strangely contradictory character constantly appears and reappears.   Simple, lovable in his
personality, abstruse and a veritable megalomaniac in his music,
one comes to take a surprising interest in this peculiar dual
nature of "Father" Heinrich.   Anton Philipp Heinrich was
born in Bohemia in 1781, coming to America for the first time
in the early eighteen hundreds, whither after several years in
England and on the continent he returned and finally settled in
New York.   Here he poured forth his soul in those remarkable
compositions which have been the amazement and despair of all
who have studied them.   He died in New York in 1861.

Let us quote two characteristic titles: "The Ornithological
Combat of Kings; or the Condor of the Andes and the Eagle of

the Cordilleras. Comprising firstly the Conflict in the Air, secondly the Repose, thirdly the Battle for Victory on Land. Concerto Grosso Oratoriale. Orchestral with Vocal Illustrations." Second title: "Nec plus ultra, Yankeedoodleiad, Toccata Grandissima Americana. Dedicated to his Majesty Friedrich Wilhelm IV, King of Prussia, etc. etc. etc." Was ever such grandiloquence! Such naïve and indiscriminate manufacture of nondescript words! And these often coupled with personal comments and explanations so simple and modest that they form a perfect antithesis both to the title that precedes and the music that follows. A strange combination!

Notice must also be taken of various men whose work appears in purely fragmentary manner in the copyright issues of this period, and of whom we know little or nothing; yet who showed ability to do things out of the ordinary everyday way. Their names at least should not be forgotten. George P. H. Loder, brother-in-law of Henry C. Watson and Conductor of the New York Philharmonic Society, published in 1840 *Touch Us Gently, Time* and *Ossian's Glen*, both skilful, musicianly songs. Elam Ives, Jr. (1802-1864), one time Principal of the Philadelphia Musical Seminary, published at Philadelphia, probably in the late thirties or early forties, a sacred duet, *Behold the Gentle Dew*, which is really good, with imitative work in the voice parts and an interesting accompaniment. William A. King, of English birth but whose musical career seems to have been made in America and who was organist at Grace Church, New York, for sixteen years, published in 1843 the song *Love's Faith*, in broad, effective style, but with some peculiarly unvocal effects, as for instance:
heav - ing
also an *Ave Maria* of his was sung at a concert given by the American Musical Association in New York, June, 1857. Incidentally, it is interesting to observe the list of American com-

posers represented in the programs of this Society in 1857: Dr. Hodges, Bristow, Fry, Curtis, Mason, Pychowski, Homman, Willis, R. F. Halstead, W. A. King, A. Reiff, Jr., Appy, J. A. Johnson, Jerome, J. M. Deems, Siede, W. H. Walter. Many of these names have sunk into what is undoubtedly a well-deserved oblivion, but some of them we shall meet with later on. Charles Jarvis, prominent musician, pianist, and manager of high-grade concerts in Philadelphia for many years, published in 1846, at least in part, the romantic opera *Luli, or the Switzer's Bride*. He makes free use of accompanied recitative, simple in style, dignified in effect. *Deign, O Heaven, to hear my prayer* is straightforward, genuine, with interesting use of the minor ninth. His arias show strong Italian influence. James Flint, otherwise absolutely unknown, published in 1848 an *Anthem and Fugue* of excellent construction. In 1849, George Henry Curtis published the song *Come here, come here and dwell*, harmonically notable from the fact that he made use of the mediant modulations then first beginning to appear.

We have to chronicle during this period the death of those four mighty men of our early musical development—Carr, Taylor, Hewitt and Graupner. Peace to their ashes.

# CHAPTER IV

## 1850-1870

*Dwight's Journal, Stephen Collins Foster, William H. Fry,*

*George F. Bristow, Richard Storrs Willis, James M. Deems,*

*Francis Boott, G. W. Stratton, George F. Benkert*

WITH these years we reach that remarkable migration to Germany on the part of our young American musicians which was to have such far-reaching results and so strongly affect the progress of American music for the next half century that all other influences seemed purely negligible. France and Italy had their few disciples, but they were as nothing when compared with those who sat at the feet of the German masters. And of course this was entirely as it should be. At that time there was nothing in the entire world of music comparable to the depth and vitality of the music of Germany, nor to the thoroughgoing methods of German teaching. Mendelssohn had but recently (1843) established the Conservatory at Leipsic whose influence upon contemporary music has probably never been surpassed. Its very conservatism was perhaps an element for good just then, for holding so firm a conviction that it possessed the one and only true light in music it could not well be otherwise than zealous and persistent in its diffusion; and even in consigning to outer darkness all corners not illumined by its own particular rays, it perhaps did the world a great service; for where was there a stronger or purer light, a beacon more helpful to the seeker after musical truth? The schools of music which soon followed—the Berlin Conservatory in 1850, the Neue

Academie der Tonkunst in 1855, and the schools in Dresden and Munich received their varying quotas of American students, but through it all Leipsic reigned supreme. Only very few serious students found themselves in Florence or Paris.

Almost commensurate with this powerful influence abroad was that of *Dwight's Journal of Music* here at home. Perhaps it is not too much to say that the name of John Sullivan Dwight should be coupled with that of Theodore Thomas, as the two most influential individuals in America in our earlier days, in molding public taste, in elevating the standard of music in every possible way. The *Journal of Music* was founded in 1852 and continued until 1881. From its very outset Dwight endeavored, by precept and example, by letter-press and printed note, to teach the enlarging gospel of a true and lofty musical righteousness. Nor was he lacking in a very real newspaper sense of the value of personality in his magazine. He was vitally interested in all the musical doings about him, in the careers of serious-minded musicians everywhere, particularly of young Americans; so that not only was the *Journal* of great interest and value to its contemporaries, but to us of today it furnishes a perfect mine of information. To anyone doing research work in American music of this time its files are invaluable.

In his first issue (April 10, 1852) Dwight speaks of the re markable musical progress made in America in the last fiftee more especially the last ten years, i.e., from 1837 or 1842 to tl time of writing, 1852. He recognizes how "confused, crud heterogeneous is this sudden musical activity in a young utili tarian people." Yet we can find good omen in a program of songs by Schubert, Schumann, Mendelssohn, Fesca and Franz, quoted by him in a later issue of the same year. Fesca might seem a bit outclassed, but otherwise who can cavil at such a program, particularly in America in 1852?

It can be imagined with what a warm welcome Dwight re-

ceived the first issue by an American house of the Schubert songs
already noted.   These were followed in 1853 by a *Slumber Song*
(*La Berceuse*) and in 1855 *Eulogy of Tears* (*Lob der Thränen*)
—German at last!   Also in 1855 appeared *Mignon's Song* and
*Am Meer*.   In 1850, thanks to Jenny Lind who apparently introduced them with such success that they found immediate publication, there appeared three songs by Schumann (in German) :
*Wenn ich in Deine Augen seh'*, *Mein goldenes Ringelein* and *Die
Rose, die Lilie;* and in 1852, *Widmung*, published by Benteen
at Baltimore.   It has become the vogue recently to belittle,
somewhat, the art and the personality of Jenny Lind.   Should
we not rather be deeply grateful to her for bringing to us in
those formative days these fine examples of the very best in
German song?   And, at the same time, may we not sincerely
congratulate ourselves that our audiences were musically far
enough advanced to appreciate the real worth of these songs?
In 1855 was issued the first Franz song, *Ave Maria*, and in
1856, *The Water Lily*.   The number of these German reprints
was thus not great, but we could scarcely ask for better quality.

It now becomes possible to sum up the careers of some of
those young American musicians recently merely mentioned.   Of
these in some ways the most interesting Stephen Collins
Foster, who died in 1864, at the age of thirty-eight.   The first
song of his to appear in the copyright collection is *There's a
Good Time Coming* which was issued in 1846, when the writer
was but twenty years old.   It was followed in 1847 by *What
must a Fairy's Dream Be*, and in 1848, *Stay, Summer Breath*.
These songs show no suggestion of that homely, pathetic, quasi-
negro type which Foster was soon to make so peculiarly his own.
But in the same year (1848) appeared *Uncle Ned, O Susanna*
and *Away Down South*, the first tentative beginnings of what the
world has long since identified as the Foster type of song.   In
the very next year this became distinctive by the publication of

Foster's Ethiopian Melodies, comprising *Nelly was a Lady, My brudder gum*, and *Dolcy Jones*. That he did not at this time, however, feel himself finally committed to this type is shown by *Summer Longings*, a simple but dignified song published in this same year (1849), followed in 1850 by *Mary Loves the Flowers* and *The Voice of Bygone Days*, in the first of which Foster goes far afield for him in harmonization, touching three or four different keys and even making use of sequence. On the other hand these were followed by *Old Folks at Home*, and in 1853 *My old Kentucky Home* and *Massa's in de Cold, Cold Ground* were published. Dwight's *Journal* in its issue of October 2, 1852 remarks that everybody is singing *Old Folks at Home*, little thinking, probably, that the same could be said with equal truth some three quarters of a century later! Still another zigzag and in 1854 we find in *Jeanie with the Light Brown Hair* the almost inconceivable fact of a touch of coloratura in a Foster song! In 1857 appeared *I See Her Still in My Arms* in which occurs what seems the one and only bit of independent melodic writing in the accompaniment of any Foster song.

As to Foster's place in the development of indigenous art-song it is difficult to speak. He seems to have been of a sensitive, introspective nature, to have written his own texts from such a sense of the difficulty of unifying words and music that he felt it necessary that both originate in the same source; and he seems to have worked over and over these original texts with the utmost pains. All this shows the spirit of conscious and conscientious art. Harold Milligan, in his study of Foster, probably speaks to the point when he says, "If art is an attempt of the human spirit to express itself in its relation to life, and if simplicity of means, as well as lucidity, are to be accounted artistic virtues, then *Old Folks at Home* must remain for all times one of the greatest achievements of musical art." And he also appears to have summed up this situation well in sug-

gesting that Foster's career is a good example of what happens
when a musical temperament is associated with unmusical environment.   It is conceivable that had he been placed in more
musical atmosphere, with better opportunities for musical culture, he might have developed into one of our great writers in
the larger, more elaborated art-forms.   On the other hand, a
genius is a genius, no matter where he may be placed; and we
may probably best think of Foster as standing quite apart from
the main current of conscious art-song with which we are primarily concerned, but with a dignity and worth all his own, the
true embodiment of the spirit of our people in spontaneous song.

A musician of very different type was William H. Fry, born
in Philadelphia in 1813, died the same year as Foster, 1864.
Aggressive, opinionated, egotistical, but also possessed of very
real musical gifts, a skilful writer and critic, a man of the world,
educated abroad, with six years in Paris where he was a friend
of Berlioz, a brave fighter for his ideals, albeit at times a very
quixotic one, perhaps the most quarreled with musician of his
time in America, Fry is a fascina    study for any biographer.
In the eyes of his contemporaries:     hould like him but disagree with him" (Dwight, 1853); "    lendid frigate at sea
without a helm" (Willis, 1854); and 1    eyes of us of the
twentieth century, an inconsistent but m    ent fighter for
the right, as he saw the right, in the mu     fairs of his
ountry.

In 1854, Fry gave to the *Musical World and Times* (N. Y.),
in its issue of January 21, of that year, a complete statement of
his views on musical art, particularly as it concerned America.
Here he pleaded for independence in our music, that we should
follow no man's lead.   It is a long, rambling thesis, yet of ab-
sorbing interest in view of its time and place.   In view, too, of
later developments, it is interesting to read what he has to say of
"mystic harmonies" and the like.   He was probably the first in

America to deliver a series of lectures on the history of the development of music. These were given in New York, on a lavish scale, to audiences literally numbering thousands. He made use of rich illustrative material, employing the best performers available for the purpose, even including a full orchestra. So great was the success of this venture that he was asked to repeat it in other cities. A man apparently of great personal magnetism, it is perhaps to be doubted whether his learning in these matters was commensurate with his ambitions. But at any rate he made people think.

His early opera *Leonora*, the first American opera of the modern type, although written years before and produced in Philadelphia, did not reach New York until March 29, 1858, when Fry was forty-five years of age. This opera is really a landmark in American music. Fortunately a complete copy still exists in the Library of Congress. Written along Italian lines throughout, it is dramatically conceived, with portions of very real power and effectiveness, and is apparently vastly superior to anything of its kind at that time written in America. For the most part its accompanied recitatives are skilfully handled, although the arias follow the Italian custom in being generally overdecorated. There are, however, various excellent ensemble effects.

A second opera, *Esmeralda* (*Notre Dame de Paris*), was also first produced in Philadelphia, May 2, 1864, under the directio of Theodore Thomas. It is said that Patti volunteered to sing its chief role in Europe, but satisfactory arrangements could not be made for production there. Fry also wrote various symphonies and a *Stabat Mater*, but, as far as we know, no detached songs. A duet (*Cujus Animam*) from the *Stabat Mater* is extant and shows his prevailing fault of overelaboration, although here too there are moments of true effectiveness. Fry seems always to have thought in the large. He might well be called the American Berlioz, as there are striking points of similarity in their personalities and careers. It was apparently not for nothing that the two were real friends.

The careers of William H. Fry and George F. Bristow seem always vitally associated although Bristow was born in 1825 in Brooklyn, where he died in 1898, thus outliving Fry by some thirty odd years. But their mature careers were essentially contemporary, and they were the two outstanding Americans of their time in the same field—that of the symphony and opera. Yet two personalities more utterly unlike could scarcely be imagined. Where Fry was dominating, Bristow was almost timid; Fry egotistical, Bristow modest and self-effacing; Fry brilliant, dramatic, Bristow slow and plodding. And yet there is a solidity of workmanship in Bristow's best writing to which in all probability Fry never attained. There is now no opportunity for studying the orchestral scores of either of these two men, and Bristow's opera *Rip van Winkle* (first performed in 1855) is available only in part; all trace of his oratorio, *Daniel*, has disappeared, as also of the Cantata *Niagara*, performed shortly before his death by the New York Manuscript Society amidst great public enthusiasm. But there are preserved for us his oratorio *Praise to God*, Op. 33, performed in New York and published by Ditson in 1867, and many of his songs. The opera, *Rip van Winkle*, shows his almost complete lack of any dramatic sense and in this respect is not comparable with Fry's work along this line. But his so-called oratorio (which is rather a setting of the text of the *Te Deum*) probably goes deeper than anything of Fry's. It is scholarly writing of the Mendelssohn school and is technically very well done. As would perhaps be expected from such influence, it is not striking in its originality either of conception or execution, but it is serious and worthy religious music.

Perhaps the one element in Bristow's music that still attracts

us most is his keen sense of harmonic color.  In the same first
issue of Dwight's *Journal* from which we have already quoted,
the editor, speaking of the changes that had taken place in
music during the last few years, refers particularly to the important modification of the modulatory scheme, now often turning toward the mediant keys instead of always toward the
dominant and subdominant as heretofore.  Bristow, from his
very earliest published work, makes skilful use of this novel
modulatory procedure.  His first song, *Thine Eye hath Seen
the Spot* (1846), is a simple, genuine kind of song, but shows
this unusual richness of color, passing through the keys of $G$, $B\flat$,
$D\flat$, and making use of the enharmonic $C\sharp$—$D\flat$ in passing from
the key of $D\flat$ back to $D$.  All of this was quite unusually rich
and effective, a distinctly new note in American music of that
day.

Thine Eye Hath Seen the Spot — Bristow

rayed,———— Bloom o'er the hal - low'd earth,———— where our dear in - fant's laid.——

The *Welcome Back* (1848) shows a similar modulation from $A\flat$ to *C*. *I Would I Were a Favorite Flower* (1850) gives us a ⅜ climax chromatically introduced, that device so characteristic of German composers of the romantic school; and *Spring Time is Coming* (1852) is also unusually effective in its climax by

Spring Time is Coming—Bristow

(10)

Love - ly na - ture seems to fling.. All— her charms With

will - ing arms    In the lap— of bloom - ing spring.—

reason of the strongly dissonant appoggiatura employed, and an interesting modulation is made from *A* to *F*.

(11)           Spring Time is Coming—Bristow

Her   song   of  re - joi   cing  to

Note, too, the refinement of this progression from the introduction:

It is nothing to us today, but at that time it meant much. Dwight reviews this song in his issue for November 6, 1852, referring to the delicate charm of its melody and its picturesque and graceful accompaniment.

Bristow studied with MacFarren in London.

Another contemporary, but outliving both Fry and Bristow,

was Richard Storrs Willis, born in Boston, 1819, died in Detroit, 1900. Willis enjoys the distinction of having been the first American to go to Germany to study music. When he went in 1841, after his studies at Yale where he had taken a prominent part in all musical activities, the Leipsic Conservatory was not yet founded and he went to Frankfort-on-Main to study harmony and form with Schnyder von Wartensee. Later he had counterpoint and instrumentation with Hauptmann at Leipsic. On his return to America he was very influential as editor of various leading musical periodicals. It was he who as editor of the *Musical World and Times* (New York) in 1854 opened its columns to Fry for his much-discussed confession of faith already referred to, with the result that the two men, looking at things from quite different angles, carried on a spirited newspaper controversy which lasted a long time, absorbed much paper and ink, and, as is usual in such cases, ended by leaving the two opponents exactly where they stood at the beginning. But it was highly stimulating to all concerned and probably worth while.

Willis wrote numerous songs which appeared from time to time in his magazines, showing good taste and excellent workmanship. They were always simple and unpretentious. Perhaps *Sleep, the Kind Angel is Near Me* (1849) is as typical of his style as any, but note the unusual augmented triad. In the *Musical World* in 1859 he published a sort of song-cycle consisting of three songs, *March*, *April*, and *May*, having optional modulatory connections. The first is simple, with a good theme; the second makes clever thematic use of the descending form of the *E major* scale and has an interesting modulation from *E* to *C*; the third is more elaborate, with recitative and air, the former characterized by the excellence of its declamation. Willis' memory is kept green for us of today through his admir-

Sleep the Kind Angel is Near Me — Willis

1. Soft - ly I rest on his bo - som,
2. Death, the kind an - gel, is near__ me!

Trust - ing in hopes that are o'er!__
An - gel of balm and of rest!__

able setting of *It came upon a midnight clear*—still popular and much sung at Christmas time.

Almost exactly contemporary with Willis, although of different type, is James M. Deems, born 1818 at Baltimore, where

May — Willis

Dream-like your beau-ty,    Still,   se-ques-tered

*Recit. ad lib.*

groves!    Your soft, spring ver-dure    close-ly    shuts me in.

Dense are these leaf-y    shades,    'Mid float-ing clouds    of loos-en'd

blos-soms    and be - wil - der-ing scents    en - tranced I. wan-der!

he died 1901.   He, too, studied abroad, wrote an opera *Esther*,
as well as an unfinished opera, *The Unbidden Guest*, an oratorio,
*Nebuchadnezzar*, also numerous instrumental compositions and
songs.   All traces of the larger works seem to have been lost;
the songs remaining are of very light calibre, although in his
first published song, *May I Hope to Call Thee Friend* (1844),
with "cornopean and piano accompaniment," the cornopean part

May I Hope to Call Thee Friend—Deems

name,        As— friend, dear— friend to me.

is fairly independent, following the voice neither in melody nor
rhythm, thus giving evidence of real ability and musicianship
on the part of the composer.

Contemporary with all these men, ~ster, Fry, Bristow,
Willis and Deems, even born the same yea~         ~13) but
dying in 1904, at the ripe age of ninet~            ~orty years
later than Fry and outliving them          ~ ~oott stands
quite apart in every respect fr~    ~roup of   ~ntempor-
aries.   His only resemblanc~    ~ith Foster, in t~    ~ey both
~rote nothing but songs, and that prolifically.  ~    ~radu-
~ted at Harvard in 1831, later going to Italy for st~    ~ will
~e remembered that these were the years in which Ita~an influence was at its height in America, when the supreme effort
was being made to supplant English opera—ballad-opera—with
that from Italy.   The only Americans who seem to have yielded
whole-heartedly to this appeal were Francis Boott and later Harrison Millard).   Boott studied with Picchianti at Florence and
made his home in that city for many years, returning to America
in 1875.   During this time, however, various of his songs were

published in America. The six songs appearing in 1846 under the pen name "Telford" are quite undistinguished. Somewhat better are the eight songs issued in 1857 under the general caption, *Florence*, and comprising the following titles: *Sands O' Dee* (Kingsley), *Stars of the Summer Night* and *The Night is clear and cloudless* (Longfellow), *Ring out wild Bells*, and *Break, break, break, on thy Cold Grey Stones, O Sea* (Tenny-

Sands O'Dee — Boott

(15)

3. Oh! is it weed, or fish, or float - ing hair? A tress o' gold - en hair, O' drown - ed maid - en's hair, A - bove the nets at sea? Was

son), *From the Close-shut Window* (Lowell), *Battle of the Baltic* (Campbell), and *I am Weary with Rowing* (author not given). In the first of these songs, *Sands O' Dee*, the constantly recurring three-fold repetition in the text is interestingly mirrored in the music, and the entire song is simple and effective. The songs in general, however, lack individuality, the quieter ones being distinctly the best. The accompaniments are commonplace, with little harmonic interest. At times a bit of imitation arouses hope of some interesting treatment, but it is never carried to a finish. Dwight refers to these songs in his issue of June 13, 1857 as "not strikingly original, but graceful and facile, much to be preferred to the popular sweetish, sentimental type," an eminently fair appraisal.

Boott's choice of texts, however, was always admirable, seeming to embrace the entire literary world—the best English and American poets rubbing elbows with those of Spain, France, Germany and Italy, either in translation or the original form, thus betokening broad literary culture on the part of their composer. Some of the songs issued at a much later period, although probably written earlier than their published date, show increased ability, such as *Gastibelza* (from Victor Hugo), 1885, effective in its grim simplicity; *Jenny kissed me* (Leigh Hunt), 1887, with a touch of imitation between voice and piano; and *The Bell Buoy* (Kipling), 1901, dignified, straightforward and catching well the spirit of the poem.

Two other names should perhaps be mentioned here, G. W. Stratton and George F. Benkert. The former, in the fashion of his time, wrote "tragic operas" and fairy operettas, besides many songs. These are of no outstanding value, and yet the man who in the year 1850 could write the following passage in the song *My Heart's Queen*, must have had something to say.

Here was the duo-planed music of the future definitely foreshadowed! There is something decidedly heartening in the way

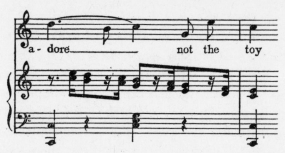

a - dore not the toy

in which these two themes march obstinately side by side, ignoring each other absolutely except for one rather wicked dig in the ribs! Another song, *My Eulalie* (1860) has an interesting postlude, and at one point a brief moment of individuality in the bass. The other songs are of no real consequence.

George F. Benkert spent five years in Germany, and a Mass of his is said to have been performed with great success under Hellmesberger in Vienna, with orchestra and a chorus of a hundred voices. His chief importance in our eyes, perhaps, lies in the fact that he was the teacher of John Philip Sousa, who, according to Rupert Hughes, considers him one of the most complete musicians our country has ever known. His first song (at the age of eighteen), *Look Not*, is of no interest, while *Pretty Jenny Wren* of the next year, 1850, although simple, shows more individuality. *Grüss Gott* (1857) is a good, musicianly song containing some excellent part writing.

# CHAPTER V

## 1850-1870 (CONTINUED)

*Lucien H. Southard, J. C. D. Parker, Alfred H. Pease,*

*Harrison Millard, Benjamin E. Woolf, Louis Moreau*

*Gottschalk, B. D. Allen, J. Remington Fairlamb, B. J. Lang,*

*Richard Hoffmann, S. B. Mills, Otto Dresel, Wulf Fries,*

*Gustav Satter, Frederic Brandeis, S. B. Schlesinger,*

*Joseph Mosenthal, Karl Merz, Julius Eichberg,*

*Frederick L. Ritter, Robert Goldbeck*

IT would seem that with the next group to be studied—L. H. Southard, J. C. D. Parker, Alfred H. Pease, and their contemporaries—we may fairly feel that we have reached the real beginnings of art-song in America. In fact we might almost be tempted to say that American song begins with J. C. D. Parker's imaginative setting of Tennyson's *Come into the Garden, Maud.* Perhaps, however, that is too broad a statement to go unchallenged, too specific to be historically verified. But at least we may take it as our text.

Lucien H. Southard (1827-1881) published his first song, *David's Lament for Absalom,* in 1848, at the age of twenty-one. While seriously treated and sincere, it fails to equal some of his later songs. *The Little Sleeper* (J. Clement), published in 1852, is notable for its accompaniment which, contrary to all the custom of the time, is full (perhaps overfull) and elaborate. In fact it rather overbalances the voice part and tends to destroy the equilibrium of the song. But as hinting at the future development of the accompaniment in the modern art-song, it is of very real historical interest.

The Little Sleeper—Southard

The song shows various artistic effects, such as slight imitative touches, refined harmonization, and the unusual effect at that time of the reentrance of the voice before the piano interlude had finished. All these evidences of good taste and musicianship make it a notable song for its time. It is quite possible that this song and *The Fountain* (Lowell), 1855, might well challenge the distinctive place assigned above to Parker's song. *No More* (W. W. Story), 1858, has bits of graceful melody in the piano score. *The Sands o' Dee* (Kingsley), 1872, shows identical rhythms for the threefold repetition in the text, but not, as was the case in Boott's setting of this same poem, the same melody. *The Tryst* (S. P. Driver), 1873, has a charming four measure obbligato in the accompaniment, the whole song being simple and lyric. *O Moonlight Deep and Tender* (Lowell) makes use of the interesting progression from $C$ to $A^b$, and is more varied in its expression than some of Southard's songs. The songs in general are characterized by delicacy and refinement, but show only the faint beginnings of modern harmonization and but slight attempts at independence in the accompaniment; they are sometimes awkward in declamation, but always show dignity of style and true musicianship.

As far as we know, J. C. D. Parker (1828-1916) wrote but the one song, *Come into the garden, Maud* (1855), which Dwight in his *Journal* calls "one of the most promising songs that we have seen by any of our young composers . . . . graceful and in the setting of the last verse, especially the last two lines, happy; but the principal melody seems rather too light, and not to have seized the spirit of the words." Here more Dwight shows himself a discriminating critic, and with final sentence might seem to have quite demolished our thesis. But, granting the justice of his criticism, there is so much to admire in the rest of the song, that it still seems reasonable to assign it to its high place. At the words "the woodbine spices are wafted abroad," the thinness and openness of the accompaniment, the graceful melodic line, and the use of secondary harmonies seem to give just the right atmosphere.

Come Into the Garden, Maud — Parker

And the entire stanza

> "There has fallen a splendid tear
> From the passion flower at the gate.
> She is coming, my dove, my dear,
> She is coming my life, my fate.
> The red rose cries, 'She is near';
> And the white one weeps, 'She is late';
> The larkspur listens, 'I hear';
> And the lily whispers, 'I wait.' "

is excellently interpreted, word for word, note for note. It is admirable music at any time; for the year 1855, and from a young American, it is notable.

Come Into the Garden, Maud — Parker

**Come Into the Garden, Maud (Continued)**

With Alfred H. Pease (1838-1882), we come to the man who in one respect at least stands out from all his contemporaries— in the lavish use of a vividly tinted palette. There is no one of his time in America whose harmonic fabric is so sensuously colored. At times it is even cloying, but one feels inclined to forgive this offence in view of the meagre tonal effects to be found elsewhere. In this regard he follows in the footsteps of George F. Bristow, but goes far beyond him. He also makes much use of sequence and sometimes shows an almost French feeling for the individual and characteristic qualities of secondary harmonies. All these elements serve to take him quite off the beaten path of his time. If to these admirable qualities he could have added a keener feeling for dissonance, his harmonic effects would have gained enormously in vigor and intensity. As it is, he often charms, but rarely moves. Quite unoriginal in melody and rhythm, for the most part ineffective in his accompaniments, with almost no use of obbligato melody, he still surprises us at times with unlooked for beauties in the score. Pease gives the impression of great natural talent (particularly in a harmonic sense), either quite undisciplined, or, perhaps, erratic and not sufficiently self-critical. But that he possessed unusual gifts cannot be denied.

He spent some six years in Germany. In reporting to Dwight's *Journal* (June 8, 1859) on the various American students then in Berlin, A. W. Thayer refers to Pease, then studying at the Kullak Academy, and says he had met him once or twice, but never at the best concerts! Of course that may or may not be illuminating. Sometime later, Robert Goldbeck, Editor of the *Musical Independent,* Chicago, in its issue for April, 1871, says, "There is no doubt that Mr. Pease is perhaps the most effective concert pianist our city possesses." In this connection we may note that he played his own *Piano Concerto in E♭* at an all-American concert given by Theodore Thomas in

Philadelphia, July 19, 1876.   Other numbers on the program were Fry's Pastoral Overture *A Day in the Country* and J. K. Paine's Symphony in *C minor*.   We see that our composer-pianist finds himself in good company.   In his issue for November, 1872, Goldbeck says (referring this time to Pease primarily as a composer), "I believe there is a future for him.   Experience is fast supplying the absence of former thorough study.   Still we ought to remind Mr. Pease that he is not yet entirely free from crudities."   In spite of these crudities and inequalities, however, the songs of Pease offer a most interesting field for study.

Pease seems to have published his first songs in 1864, and from that time until his death in 1882 there was scarcely a year without some new song from his pen.   His first published songs were *When Sparrows Build* (Jean Ingelow) and *Blow, Bugle, Blow* (Tennyson).   In the latter song we see at once his fondness for the mediant harmonic relationship, for sequence and the like.

(19)                                        Blow, Bugle, Blow—Pease

How sweet and far, from cliff and scar, The horns of

Elf - land faint - ly blow - ing.

In 1865 came three of his most interesting songs: *Stars of the Summer Night* (Longfellow), with its smoothness and gentle lyricism, its rich color, its fleeting suggestions of obbligato melody, even a touch of discreet dissonance;

Stars of the Summer Night — Pease

(20)

Stars of the sum-mer night! Far in yon

az - ure deeps,___ Hide, hide your gold-en light! She
sleeps!___ my_ la - dy sleeps! sleeps!_ sleeps!

*Tender and True, Adieu*, with a more mediocre text than we ordinarily find with Pease, is still treated with very real skill. The rather extended prelude is romantic in spirit, exceedingly interesting and effective. It gives the key to the whole song.

Tender and True Adieu— Pease

(21)   Moderato

The recurrence of various motifs in the course of the song gives unity and cohesion. For its time it is distinctly a notable piece of work. In the third song, *A Year's Spinning* (Elizabeth Barret Browning), the inevitable descriptive elements are well handled. *Good Night* (T. B. Aldrich), 1866, is particularly happy in its use of secondary harmonies. The *Cradle Song* (Tennyson's *Sweet and Low*), 1867, makes use of an obbligato melody in the accompaniment. In Bells (Amelia B. Edwards), 1869, we find one of those unlooked for, musicianly touches which, as we have said, crop out unexpectedly here and there in his songs —in this instance the unusual and irregular stroke of the bells, which occurs on the first, sixth and fourth beat of a two-measure phrase in six eight time. It is as felicitous as it is unexpected. Unfortunately the melodic value of this song is slight. Of 1870 there are two songs: first, a ballad, *Darling, Kiss my Eyelids Down*, interesting only as it follows in its structure a familiar Schubert model: major, parallel minor, relative major to this minor, original major—in this case, *A major, A minor, C major, A major;* second, *Dreamland (Sleep, Baby, Sleep*, from the German), in which the composer makes free use of secondary sevenths. *Douglas, Tender and True* (Miss Mulock), 1872,

shows a clever touch in that the interlude following the words
"tender and true" is reminiscent of the melody accompanying
these same words in the earlier song, *Tender and True, Adieu.*

I *Love my Love* (Charles Mackay), of the same year, has elaborate cadenzas, unusual in his songs, and *O My Maid is Fairer*

*Still* (also 1872) is a deft and buoyant arrangement of a Hungarian air. Another setting of *Sleep, Baby, Sleep*, this time for two voices (1874), shows frequent use of sequence and a somewhat tentative obbligato in the accompaniment. Other songs issued in 1874 were *O, if My Love would come to Me*, simple, but catching the mood of the text better than some of his songs and with an arpeggiated accompaniment unusual for Pease,

Oh, If My Love Would Come to Me — Pease

(24)

O, if my love would come to me, And hold my hands and look at me, The while he lov-ing spoke to me, My life would so much bright-er be.

also *Love's Good Morrow*, one of the composer's few florid songs.
*Just as of Old* (1875) shows overuse of sequence, *My Little
Love* (1878), intelligent appreciation of secondary harmonies,
*To the Queen's Health* (Thomas Bailey Aldrich), of the same
year, unusually vigorous rhythm and an eight-measure sequence.
*Slumber Sweetly*, published in the very year of his death, 1882,
discloses once more his fondness, perhaps overfondness, for sequence.   We shall have occasion to recur to this subject of
sequence when we come to discuss the songs of Homer N. Bartlett.

We find, then, in these songs of Pease many suggestions of
the technique which was to come to maturity soon after his time
—more especially in his free use of deceptive cadence, of sequence, pedal-point, and enharmonic modulation; less distinc-
tively in his rather reserved treatment of dissonance, his slight
employment of counter melody in the accompaniment, and of
imitative work generally.   But most vividly of all we have seen
that love of romantic color which definitely sets him apart from
 ` fellows and establishes his kinship with the future.

  'ontemporary with this group, but apart from it, just as
ᴸ       Boott stood apart from the earlier group, is Harrison
Miⅼ       ʹ1830-1895), and for the identical reason that they
both ᵪ      ᵉd their musical education in Italy.   Millard was a
professiᵤ      ʹnger and his songs are the songs of a singer rather
than those o̱  ᵢ musician.   His first published song, *The Kind
Word* (1848), is of little or no significance.   Beginning with
this song published at the age of eighteen, there poured on
through the years a ceaseless stream of songs.   Varying somewhat in value, but all built on substantially the same plan, these
songs make no essential contribution to American song.   With
no harmonic interest, no individual piano score, they depend
entirely upon their melodic line for any value they may possess.
Mozart could on occasion write an air with the simplest possible

The Pretty Zingarella—Millard

(25)

Of-ten in Spain, the Zin - - ga - rel - la

Dan-ces with glee, to plain - tive_ tune.

harmonization and the thinnest possible accompaniment, an air which would still sing itself down the ages; but unfortunately Millard was no Mozart. His songs, no doubt, fitted the temper of their time; it is certain that they had a great vogue. On his return from Italy where he spent the years 1851 to 1854, he sang in concert, among other things, his own song *La Domanda,* which Dwight characterizes (November 10, 1855) as a "melody which well hits the average style of current Italian melody, and of course well suited to his own voice." In general that is a fair estimate of his large output of literally hundreds of songs.

To this time also belong Louis Moreau Gottschalk (1829-1869), B. D. Allen (1831-1914), J. Remington Fairlamb (1837-1908), and B. J. Lang (1837-1909), all excellent and influential musicians, the two last named with thorough European training, but none of them of any outstanding importance in the development of American song.

Aside from this group of native-born Americans there are still some coming from across the sea. England who played so predominant a role in our earlier musical development is now much less fully represented, while the influence of Germany constantly increases. From England came Richard Hoffmann, born 1831, coming to America 1847, died 1909; B. E. Woolf, born 1836, America 1839, died 1901; S. B. Mills, born 1838, America 1859, died 1898. Richard Hoffmann and S. B. Mills, while distinguished in other directions, have no decisive bearing upon our particular subject. If they wrote any songs they have been lost sight of in the greater significance of their work along other lines. Benjamin E. Woolf, however, along with his other musical and literary activities, wrote numerous songs. Coming to America at three years of age, he is perhaps rather to be classed among the native Americans than as an outsider. His songs show musical feeling and refinement of style, which unfortunately often outrun his technical ability. He was apparently fond of independent melodies in the piano score, which he used with considerable skill. *How Many Times Do I Love Thee, Dear* (1884) is probably his best song. It is of interesting texture, simple and sincere. *Love Song of Har Dyah* (1894) shows oriental color, with a characteristic motif running throughout the song. *Forever* (1894) is also characterized by a recurring motif based on the first phrase of the voice part, thus imparting unity to the song.

The list of those coming from Germany at this time is a long one, headed by Otto Dresel, to whom reference has already been made. That a man of his recognized high standing, a pupil of Hiller and Mendelssohn, an intimate friend of Robert Franz, with all the idealism of a cultured German musician of that time, should come to America and give himself so devotedly to the task of helping her along the rough path of her musical development, was worth more than we can well express. His almost forty

years in Boston furnished an influence second to none in making
her the musical centre that she became. He wrote only some
twenty songs all told, but all are of a high order. In 1855 appeared two songs, both written under rather interesting circum-
stances. *Sweet Echo, Sweetest Nymph,* text from Milton's
*Comus,* was written, Dwight says (August 18, 1855), "to help
out a parlor performance of the Mask by some young people in
one of our cultured families." He characterizes the song as
"refreshingly pure and true in the way of songs," which it certainly is; dignified, sincere, and particularly effective in its
appropriate use of the echo motif. The second song, a setting
of Tennyson's *Sweet and Low,* won the first prize of two hundred
dollars in a great competition of some four hundred entries,
which called forth the sardonic scorn of our friend Dwight because of its democratic method of procedure, in that the prize
winner was not determined by the vote of competent judges but
by what amounted to universal suffrage. Under these circum-
stances we are rather inclined to share his surprise that the best
song won! He quite vindicates his position by noting that the
song that won second place, *My Gentle Mother's Song* by C. C.
Converse, was "commonplace enough," and that the really next
best song, *The Baby,* by B. D. Allen, received but one vote. In
1858 appeared Dresel's setting of *Come*
and it is interesting to compare it with Parker's setting (1855)
which we recently considered. Incidentally, how appealing these
Tennyson texts seem to have been in those years, and naturally
enough. Imagine the zest of setting such poems in the first
bloom of their appearance, before time has staled their freshness. These two settings are so entirely different, however, that
it is difficult to compare them. Where Parker's is "through-
composed," Dresel's is strophic; and of course this fundamental
difference in treatment influences the entire result. Dresel's
setting is lyric throughout, even going so far as to omit in its

entirety the dramatic stanza which forms the emotional climax
of Parker's song.   Dresel's first melody (in this case the prevailing one) is much more appropriate to the text than Parker's,
yet the cadence of the first stanza, "I am here at the gate alone,"
is much inferior.   Dresel, however, makes excellent use of altered
harmonies, with a skilfully managed sequence in which the melody remains constant while the harmonic progressions vary.   The
accompaniment is pianistic throughout, with arpeggios in sixths
and such like.   Dresel's songs were gathered together in one
volume and published by Breitkopf and Härtel in 1892.

From Wulf Fries, 'cellist, member for twenty-three years of
the well-known Mendelssohn Quintette Club which did so much
to make the better class of chamber music known in America,
and who came to America in 1847, the year before Dresel, only
one song has come down to us—the ballad *By the Stream a
Youth was Sitting* (*Der Jüngling am Bache*).   It is distinguished for its use of imitation in the bass of the accompaniment.   Also Gustav Satter, the able pianist and eccentric
gentleman, who spent parts of the years 1854 to 1860 in America
and who wielded much influence through his piano playing,
published two songs, *Constancy*, Op. 11 (1856), and *Cicily*,
Op. 12 (1857).   The former is particularly rich in its harmonization, making effective use of enharmonic modulation, and has
a rousing ⅜ climax.   In the latter song the composer very skilfully reflects in the accompaniment the words "Up, up, up in
the sky."   The punctuation and idea of gradual ascent are
picturesquely delineated.   In *Six Songs*, published later in
Vienna, Satter still more fully discloses his very real musicianship.

The influence of these two men was of course merely a fleeting one as compared with that of Dresel or others whose output
was larger.   Frederic Brandeis, coming to America from Vienna

in 1849, published in 1852 a song, *Was it a Crime to Love Thee*, which is a really remarkable song for a youth of seventeen. The harmony is interesting, the accompaniment individual. *Lady Bird*, Op. 66, No. 1 (1881), is a fittingly dainty song, with rather unusual use of the seventh on the second degree and an accompaniment figure,

rendered notable by the novel use of the repeated *e* in the left hand. *The Miller's Daughter* (Tennyson), 1883, shows a graceful, pianistically effective postlude, cleverly based on the theme of the prelude, but in diminution. *My Love is Like the Red, Red Rose*, Op. 26, (Burns), 1886, has a rich, full piano score, the accompaniment sometimes following the line of the voice, sometimes giving nothing but supporting chords, but always with distinctly clever craftsmanship. Brandeis is fond of long postludes, interesting in themselves, but dangerous to the unity of the song.

A year later than Brandeis, in 1850, Sebastian Benson Schlesinger, born in Germany in 1837, came to America as German Consul; he died in 1917 in France. While in America he took an active part in musical affairs and wrote many songs which are entirely typical of the time. Well written, according to the prevailing idioms of the day, they strike no individual note, and are no better, no worse, than many other contemporary German songs, for German they are to the core. Perhaps his most successful song, according to present-day standards, is the setting of Lingg's *Immer leiser wird mein Schlummer* (immortalized by Brahms), one of his earliest songs, 1882. While not realizing in any sense the poignancy of the text, it yet shows refined feeling and delicacy of line.

In 1853 came Joseph Mosenthal, born in 1834 at Kassel,

died, New York, 1896.    Mosenthal had been a pupil of Louis
Spohr and was a well-trained musician.    The few songs of his
which we know, as for instance, the *Three Songs* (1869):
*Heavenly Rest on Earth Descendeth* (Reinick), *Spring Has
Newly Come to Greet Us* (Otto Roquette), and *We Wandered
through the Flow'ry Vale* (Titus Ulrich) show good craftsmanship and an interesting feeling for harmonic color, and, particularly in the last named, fancy and imagination.

Karl Merz (born in Germany, 1836, died, Wooster, Ohio,
1890), came to America in 1854.    Through his teaching and
editorial work he made a truly valuable contribution to his time;
a fact which one would scarcely suspect from his songs which
were of the then prevailing type, ballads, waltz-songs, Scotch
and Tyrolean songs, and the like.    Occasionally he gave of his
best in songs more true to the German ideal, such as *I dream of
Thee* (1857) and *Stranger's Love* (*Des Fremden Liebe*), 1858,
which though simple, almost elementary, are at least dignified
and sincere, free from the trivialities that so often mar his other
songs.    *Deserted* (1873), dedicated to Annie Louise Cary, is
one of his better songs, with expressive use of the minor ninth.

The year 1856 brought two men of outstanding ability and
influence, Julius Eichberg and Frederick Louis Ritter.    The
former, born in Düsseldorf, 1824, died, Boston, 1893, was distinguished primarily for his light operas—his *Doctor of Alcan-
tara* having had a phenomenal success; the latter, best known
as teacher and writer, still found time to write many worth-while
songs.    Ritter was born at Strassburg, 1834; and died at
Antwerp, 1891.    His songs are always true to the German type
and show a decided Brahms influence.    His early song *Elfen-
liebe*, Op. 4 (1867), betrays this influence unmistakably in the
simultaneous use of two conflicting rhythms—six beats in the
voice part against four in the accompaniment—and this opposition reappears in a peculiarly Brahmsian manner in the post-

lude. Of his *Six Songs*, Op. 6 (1870), the last three are the most interesting. *Die Wasserlilie* (No. 4) has a powerful imitative climax in the middle and an attractive echo effect at the close, the voice ending in the minor, echoed by the accompaniment in the major. *Bitte* (No. 5) is excellent in its free declamation, while *Kriegertod* (No. 6) makes use of a galloping rhythm which is given a touch of originality by beginning off the beat instead of on it. The first two of *Fünf Lieder*, Op. 10 (1876), are both good. *Der schwere Abend* is again like Brahms in its modified strophic form and syncopated bass, while *Ruhe in der Geliebten* reminds us of Mendelssohn and Schumann in the use of a compact accompaniment which closely follows the voice. There is a piece of admirable part-writing in the middle section of the last stanza, where three distinct melodies are interwoven, the accompaniment here being richly scored and entirely differentiated from the voice. The second of *Four Songs*, Op. 20 (1888), *At Thy Dear Feet O Let me Lie* shows one of Brahms' favorite devices in the expansion of the cadence at the end of the second stanza. Indeed it ꞏ ꞏ song, technically at least, after Brahms' own heart, for it als. ꞏꞏates ⅔ and ⅜ rhythms and is written in modified strophic for. all these devices we see the skilfully trained musician. The w ꞏ nship is excellent, the songs attractive. It is only on the narmonic side that Ritter seems deficient, for his harmonization, while often interesting enough, is rarely outstanding.

In 1857 came Robert Goldbeck, born in Prussia, 1839, died, St. Louis, 1908. He was a nephew and pupil of Louis Köhler. His best songs are perhaps his settings of the two well-known Tennyson texts, *The Splendor Falls on Castle Walls* (1866) and *Break, Break, Break on thy Cold Grey Stones, O Sea* (1870). In the former song his innate feeling for freedom of form is of great advantage in producing appropriate dramatic effect.

The Splendor Falls on Castle Walls—Goldbeck

His alternation of ¾, ⁴⁄₄, and ⁶⁄₄ time is the first instance of such rhythmic freedom noted in American song. In fact this rhythmic variety persists throughout the entire song. In *Break, Break*, the prelude well establishes the mood, and recurs as interludes, and as a postlude. That Goldbeck had a feeling for dissonance well in advance of his time is shown in his fearless use of $e\natural$ against an *F minor* harmony. Two songs to texts by Lowell and Longfellow (1870) are somewhat less successful, although *The Day is Cold and Dark and Dreary* is excellent in its mood expression, and *O Moonlight, Deep and Tender* has some interesting harmonic progressions. In general, Goldbeck's songs are characterized by freedom of form, with numerous quasi-recitative passages, tending sometimes to awkwardness, lack of symmetry and unity, but often toward distinctly dramatic effect. His melody frequently shows chromatic character, though there is no real chromaticism in the essential harmony.

# CHAPTER VI

## 1870-1880

### *J. K. Paine, Dudley Buck, Homer N. Bartlett*

BORN the same year with Goldbeck are two well known American composers — J. K. Paine (1839-1906) and Dudley Buck (1839-1909). With the former, orchestral writing worthy the name first had its beginning in America; with the latter the same may be said as regards church music. Paine wrote few songs, Buck many. In fact, with Buck the floodgates of American song were opened and the deluge was upon us.

With Paine's orchestral writing we have nothing here to do except to pay tribute to the first American to do work of this type of really large calibre and solid workmanship. Of his few songs, representing probably the least of his musical interests, we shall, however, take brief notice. There are eight songs in all—four, Op. 29 (1879-1889) and four Op. 40 (1885).

His *Matin Song*, Op. 29, No. 1 (Bayard Taylor) 1879, is in its way a very remarkable little song. With the voice part only eighteen measures long it comprises within these limits twelve measures of absolutely different rhythms. Only the six remaining measures are permitted to show any rhythmic repetition. The result is a melodic line of great interest and spontaneity. Harmonically, the song is undistinguished. *I Wore Your Roses Yesterday* (Celia Thaxter), second of this group, is delightfully lyric and graceful, with the piano score made interesting by its unobtrusive but attractive imitative effects, while *Early Spring-time*, Op. 29, No. 3 (Rev. Thomas Hill), 1879, interests us in an entirely different way, and for its time

78

seems very revolutionary. In the first place, its text is prose—plain prose—and while it has to be admitted that Paine has not handled this unwonted declamation with complete success, still, as we should expect, there are measures of very real dignity and effectiveness. The curious thing about the song, however, is

I wore your Roses Yesterday—Paine

(27) Andante con moto

I wore your ro - ses yes - ter-day: A-
bout this light robe's folds of white, Where-
in their gath - ered sweet - ness lay, Still

that each of its two identical stanzas begins in *C♯ minor*, ends in *E major*, and then is left suspended in mid-air with a piano postlude ending in the unresolved dominant of the original *C♯ minor!* This from Paine, in America, in 1879. *The Bird upon a Rosy Bough*, Op. 40, No. 1 (Celia Thaxter), 1884, is more conventional in treatment, but is of interest by reason of its rich and sonorous piano score.

With Dudley Buck we enter upon the subject of song in America in its comparatively modern aspect, with all its nineteenth-century characteristics. And just as a moment ago it seemed the natural thing for one reason or another to bracket the names of Fry and Bristow, so in similar fashion there is a name that naturally associates itself with Buck, that of Homer N. Bartlett (1845-1911). The songs of both these men are so numerous that now for the first time in America we find opportunity for quantitative as well as qualitative study; and we may well consider that it was through their facility and fluency of expression in this form that, for better or for worse, song-writing in America became an ordinary rather than an extraordinary procedure.

Dudley Buck's first published song appeared in 1868, Homer N. Bartlett's in 1873, and from that time until practically the close of the first decade of the present century both

remained prolific song-writers. This was particularly true of
Bartlett whose opus numbers reached well into the second hundred, a dangerous circumstance it must be admitted, for where
there is such voluminous output there is sure to be inequality of
values; and this is strikingly true of Bartlett's songs. But there
is still something impressive in the mere fact that one's creative
faculty should work so unremittingly, and that there should be
a waiting public for so much iterated and reiterated expression
of one's individuality. And if one is willing to sift this mass of
material he will find certain songs of very real interest.

In the study of Bartlett's songs the characteristic that strikes
us first, last and all the time is his inordinate fondness for rich
harmonic color in connection with overfrequent use of sequence
—in both points reminding us of Alfred H. Pease. That he
could, however, use this vivid coloring with just restraint is
proven in *Her Voice to Me*, one of his best songs. In the songs
of Dudley Buck we discover evidence of an entirely different
temperament. In place of these rich harmonic sequences, attractive in themselves but repeated almost *ad nauseam* throughout the mass of Bartlett's songs, we find in Buck's songs an
equally persistent idiom, but in his case manifesting itself in a
constant restlessness of rhythm, with never any sustained effect
in the accompaniment, seldom even in the voice. The earlier
songs are characterized also by the use of most conventionally
stereotyped patterns in the piano score; indeed this style of writing continued for some thirty years. Not until 1900, or later,
was there any perceptible sign that these outworn, unoriginal
formulae were in process of dissolution. Only in the setting of
Hamlet's Soliloquy, *To be or not to be* (1903), do we begin to
see something of imaginative treatment, something of flexibility
of style.

A point of interest in regard to these two men is their opposite tendencies in the treatment of religious texts. In the case

of Dudley Buck we find his very best work in this field, while
with Bartlett the reverse is true.   With Buck, his innate feeling
for the organ, for the beauty of its smooth, sustained style,
effectually modified his ordinarily abrupt, declamatory mode of
speech, and gave to his sacred songs a dignity of expression
often lacking in his secular writing.   On the other hand, Bartlett's religious songs are for the most part just what church
music ought never to be—florid, ornate, the text and its setting
poles apart in every respect.   As showing him at his worst in
this respect, we may note the lack of taste shown in the numerous
scales, arpeggios and technical pyrotechnics of every sort which
accompany the text of *Nearer My God to Thee,* one of his
earlier settings (1883).   It may be said with something of truth
that he was merely conforming to the fashion of his time; all
the more honor, then, to Dudley Buck for rising so far above it.
Naturally Bartlett's later work showed improvement, but he
never succeeded in writing a truly sympathetic, churchly song.

Taking into account the quantity and quality of their work,
these two wr ters were undoubtedly the leading song-composers
of their ti  in America.   They each published more than fifty
songs, f   and away more than any of their contemporaries.   It
is prol   e that their methods varied as did their temperaments.
Buc'   e know, in his later years revised many of his earlier
so    nd presumably wrote with care and the requisite leisure;
Ba   tt seems to have written uninterruptedly, song after song,
on  ach the same pattern.

If we take up their songs somewhat in detail, we find in
Buck's first published song, *Where are the Swallows Fled?*
(Adelaide Proctor), Op. 36, No. 1 (1868), perhaps his most
successful use of conventional accompanying material, most successful because the simplest.   Also the first part of this song, as
often in Buck's songs, shows excellent declamation in the sense
of a melody well adapted and appropriate to the text, although

Where are the Swallows fled?—Buck

(28)

1. Where   are  the swal-lows fled?     Where   are the
2. The     sun  hath hid his rays,        The     sun hath

swal-lows fled?     Fro - - zen  and dead,
hid his rays,       These   ma - ny days,

often far from correct in its precise diction.   In this latter respect many of Buck's earlier songs are decidedly weak.   *Sunset*
(Sidney Lanier), Op. 76, No. 4 (1877) has a broadly treated
opening melody.   His setting of three Stedman poems, *Thou art
Mine, Shadow Land,* and *I Love Thee,* Op. 79 (1878, 1881),
show appropriate and effective melodies, but Buck's lack of originality and freedom in harmonic effects discloses itself more baldly
in these earlier songs.   The *Bedouin Love Song* (Bayard Taylor),
Op. 87, No. 2 (1881) is somewhat more successful, probably because Buck's strong rhythmic sense finds itself better adapted
to such a text; and with this incentive, even his harmonies suggest a greater freedom.   The three Offertories, *Judge Me, O
God, Blessed are they,* and *O Ye that Hear,* Op. 91 (1882),
make clear how great is our debt to Buck for his dignified treatment of religious texts.   The *Five Songs for Mezzo Soprano*

Sunset—Buck

Look off, dear love, a cross the sal - low sands, And mark yon meet - ing of the sun and sea; How

(1893) show a perceptible gain in flexibility in the accompaniment. It seems reasonable to suppose that his organ accompaniments for the sacred songs just mentioned, with their independent treatment of the accompanying instrument, may have called his attention to the inferiority of his piano accompaniments. At any rate from this time on he began to show improvement in this respect.   In No. 2 of this series, *Love's Remorse* (Boyle O'Reilly), Buck makes a beginning in the use of obbligato melody in the piano score.   No. 3, *Alone* (T. S. Collier), shows some thematic feeling in its cadence; while No. 4, *Spring's Awakening* (Mary E. Blake), with its elaborate recitative section has an accompaniment quite free in style;

Spring's Awakening—Buck

fret,        As it    sighs the bare boughs    fret:

unfortunately, however, the harmonization is still far from original or interesting.   No. 5, *Crossing the Bar* (Tennyson), has
even a touch of counterpoint in the piano part.   This improvement continues with *I Will Lay Me Down in Peace* (from *The
Triumph of David*) which shows something of chromaticism.   In
*Boots and Saddles* (Edna Proctor Hayes), 1901, we find much
greater freedom in the harmonization, and once more, as in the
*Bedouin Love Song*, a text favorable to Buck's rhythmic style.
We find, too, an excellent feeling for appropriate and interesting psychological treatment.   The form is free, a sort of super-
recitative, dramatically conceived.   The declamation is still
carelessly treated, however.

(31)                                        Boots and Saddles—Buck

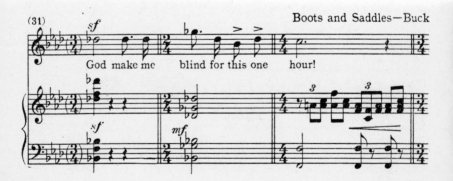

God make me    blind for this one    hour!

God_____ make me on-ly hear_____ The hur-ry-ing drum, that cry, "they come!"_____ And

*Until God's Day* (Frank L. Stanton), 1901, and *To be or not to be* (1903) give further evidence of Buck's increasing freedom of expression, the latter showing skilful declamation and appropriate recitative style.  Only Buck's unfortunate habit of over-repetition mars at times this otherwise admirable setting.  With Shakespeare's *It was a Lover and his Lass*, Frank L. Stanton's *De Gray Owl*, and *A Life Picture* (Clarence Umbry)—all of 1904—we seem to see almost entire recovery from the composer's early stiffness of manner, for here the piano score is exceedingly free and spontaneous and colorful, the whole conception more vivid and picturesque.

Spring Song—Buck

It has become increasingly apparent that there was little of the mystic, the poet, in Buck's personality, and the lack of any subjectivity in his songs is their most fundamental defect; but throughout his entire work there appears a certain straightforwardness, a virility of expression, which in the end makes its own very distinct appeal.   Apparently there is no pose, no affectation of any sort, either in the man or his music.

The songs of Homer Bartlett differ from those of Buck in many respects; in fact the two types are quite antithetical. Where Buck's harmonic sense seemed often barren and sterile, Bartlett's was oversaccharine.   Where Buck's rhythmic sense showed itself keen and virile, Bartlett's was often sluggish, inert. Buck made almost no use of sequence, that favorite device of all romantic writers; Bartlett overused it until it became nothing more than a mechanical trick, a mannerism.   We find this fact exemplified in almost his first published song, *Moonbeams* (1876).   Here we have an excellent first subject, but a superfluity of sequence and an absurdly passionate outburst on the far from dramatic concept "Social hearth"!

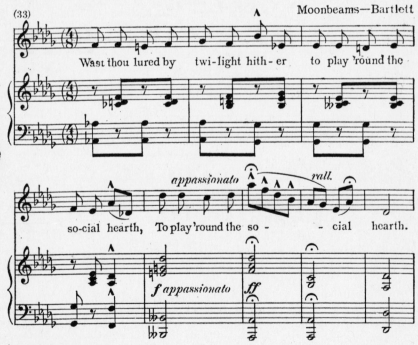

(33)        Moonbeams—Bartlett

Wast thou lured by   twi-light hith-er   to play 'round the so-cial hearth, To play 'round the so - - cial hearth.

*appassionato*     *rall.*

*f appassionato*   *ff*

It took Bartlett a long time to overcome this early tendency to theatricalism, this indiscriminate flamboyancy of style.   With *Come to me, Dearest* (Joseph Brennen), 1887, there appears a marked change of manner, unfortunately more or less temporary, so that one cannot escape the conviction that for a season our composer's writing must have come under the supervision or at least friendly criticism of some discriminating musician.   We find in this song extensive use of the chord of the seventh on the second degree over a dominant pedal-point, a distinctly new departure for Bartlett, and even some contrapuntal writing in the piano score.

(34)

Come to me, dearest—Bartlett

1. Come        to__ me, dar - ling, my sor - rows to light - en,
2. Come,        for__ my heart     in your ab - sence is wea - ry,

*marc.*

Come        in__ thy beau - ty     to bless       and     to bright - en;
Hark,        for__ my spir - it     is     sick - ened     and drear - y,

*marc.*

Copyright, 1887, by G. Schirmer

*I Hear the Brooklet Murmur* (1887) shows the same characteristics, harmonies rich but not overrich, extensive use of

Sayonara—Bartlett

(38)

Here I lie and sing no more, Sa-yo-
na-ra, Sa-yo - na - ra, With a tomb - stone for my
door, Sa-yo - na-ra, Sa-yo - na - ra. Here I

*A Song of Spring* (Lilian Pearl Turner), 1906, shows something of contrapuntal feeling, rare in these songs. *Her Voice
to Me* (John B. Bartlett), Op. 228 (1911), is probably his best

song in its free use of strong dissonance, even including the augmented triad—that, indeed, for the first time.

Her Voice to Me—Bartlett

(39)

Her voice to me, her voice to me Is full of sweet-est mel-o-dy, And thrill-ing as the morn-ing-song_____That sum-mer breez-es bear a-long, When

*Wie des Mondes Abbild* (Heine), Op. 236 (1911), seems quite inadequate, except in certain portions. Here the augmented triad appears once more. In *The Two Lovers* (Shaemas O'Sheel), Op. 237 (1911), we again find the augmented triad. 1911 seems to have been the year in which Bartlett discovered this new means of expression, and he was persistent in its use! The admirable pianistic effects in the accompaniment of this song are quite justified by their appropriateness to the "rustling grass" and "murmurs of the sea" in the text.

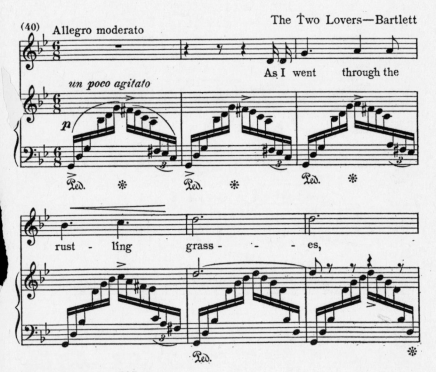

The Two Lovers—Bartlett

The passage-work in *Tell Me where is Fancy Bred* (Shakespeare), Op. 241, No. 2 (1912), is moderate in amount and not inappropriate; the change of keys is good, as is also the second subject, and the postlude is unusually effective in its combination of the two main themes. *There is a Heart* (Frederick W. Pangborn), No. 1 of the same opus, has a good opening section with broad phrasing but becomes mediocre further on. *Easter Even* (F. Whytehead), Op. 249 (1913), possesses much more of dignity than the earlier sacred songs; and his last published song, *Winds o' March* (G. Scott), Op. 272 (1920), is really an excellent song, with appropriate passage-work in the piano score and interesting harmonization.

Winds o' March—Bartlett

If Bartlett could have but exercised more severe self-criticism, could have more relentlessly pruned away the too heavy luxuriance of his harmonic style, his very real ability would have come to fuller and finer expression.

And now, before getting too far away from the subject, let us stop and consider for a moment what was the Germany of those years, 1850 to 1860 and thereabouts, to which our ambitious young American musicians were going for inspiration and training in their chosen field—Willis, Parker, Pease, Paine, and Buck.

Beethoven and Schubert had been dead some quarter of a century. Schumann, after the tragedy of his overclouding years, and Mendelssohn in the full meridian of his felicitous career had both passed on. Brahms had not yet come to the fullness of his powers. The splendor of Wagner's genius was beginning to illumine the heavens but had not yet quite pierced the fogs which lay upon the earth. There were numerous lesser musicians and composers, but what were they when compared with the giants gone or as yet unrecognized. It was the dawning of the era of the executive artist rather than the creative genius; of a Liszt rather than a Schumann past or a Brahms to come. It was the time of beginning a more or less standardized education of young musical talent, both for the concert platform and the private study, of musical education *en masse*. We have previously noted the founding of various music schools throughout Germany—at Leipsic, Berlin and other centers, and the remarkable ascendancy among them all of the Leipsic Conservatory.   Here came Willis after studying with Schnyder von Wartensee at Frankfort on the Main.   Here were J. C. D. Parker (1851-1854) and Buck (1858-1862), Parker studying under Hauptmann, Richter and Rietz, Buck under Hauptmann and Rietz, and apparently following the latter when he left Leipsic for Dresden in 1860.   Buck remained with Rietz that year in Dresden and then changed once more for Paris where he spent the year 1861.   It has been said of Hauptmann that his chief aim was to inculcate in his students the principle of "unity of idea and perfection of form," certainly a most worthy ideal and truly characteristic of Leipsic at that time.   It is not clear just what years Pease spent in Germany, although we know he was there for some six years and that he was in Berlin at the Kullak Acaden  'n 1859, where also Paine studied from 1858 to 1861.   They bᴜ  ᴡorked with Wieprecht in instrumentation; Pease with Wuerᴛ.  ᴛne with Teschner, in composition; Paine also studying orgᴜ  th Haupt, who is said to have had the distinction of teaching over thirty-five American organists.

It would perhaps be interesting also to note the foreign activities of our American singers in these same years; for we seem to have developed a really excellent group of young concert and opera singers at that time who were a distinct credit to our country.   Harrison Millard was busy with concert singing in Florence, where also Edward Sumner was singing in opera; Henry Squires, Mrs. Eastcott, and Isabella Hinkley also in opera in Italy, Mrs. Eastcott singing at Drury Lane as well; Mme. Biscaccianti, American in spite of her name, in opera throughout Europe and even in South America; Elise Hensler, soprano, and Adelaide Phillipps, contralto, both born abroad, but American from childhood, admirable and distinguished singers, the former in opera, the latter in concert and oratorio. Apparently even in these earlier years of our musical development we were ambitious for foreign laurels and fairly successful in obtaining them!

# CHAPTER VII

## 1870-1880 (Continued)

*W. K. Bassford, G. W. Marston, Oscar Weil, Stephen Emery,*

*Samuel P. Warren, George E. Whiting, George L. Osgood,*

*C. Henshaw Dana, W. W. Gilchrist, Silas G. Pratt,*

*W. J. McCoy, Louis C. Elson, N. H. Allen, Frederick Grant*

*Gleason, Jules Jordan, J. C. Bartlett, F. Q. Dulcken,*

*Clara K. Rogers, H. W. Nicholl*

WE have said that with Buck and Bartlett the flood-gates of American song were opened wide. No longer does some pianist or teacher in a moment of relaxation from his more serious labors toss off a mere song or so. Now they come rather in dozens, in fifties, in hundreds, throughout the course of one's working life. To be sure there is as yet in America no Robert Franz, no preëminent writer of songs alone. But even with us song itself has finally come to be recognized as an important element in one's creative output and seriously to be reckoned with.

Among these more or less prolific song-writers, particularly those contemporary with Buck, and thus grouped with him, we find W. K. Bassford (1839-1902), G. W. Marston (1840-1901), Oscar Weil (1840-1921), Stephen Emery (1841-1891), Samuel P. Warren (1841-1915), and George E. Whiting (1842-1923); with Bartlett, George L. Osgood (1844-1922), C. Henshaw Dana (1846-1883), W. W. Gilchrist and Silas G. Pratt (1846-1916); and a little later, W. J. McCoy (1848-

1926), Louis C. Elson (1848-1920), N. H. Allen (1848-1925), Frederick Grant Gleason (1848-1903), Jules Jordan (1850-1927), and J. C. Bartlett (1850-1929). Among those coming from England we find F. Q. Dulcken (1837-1902), Clara Kathleen Rogers (1844-), and H. W. Nicholl (1848-1922).

The songs of W. K. Bassford and G. W. Marston seem quite undistinguished. The former's early song, *Home they brought her Warrior Dead*, Op. 35 (1866) is probably his best—a simple, genuine, effective song. Oscar Weil is best known for his two excellent songs: *In Autumn* and *Spring Song*, Op. 10, Nos. 1 and 2.

Stephen Emery made interesting use of imitation between the voice and piano in *Good Night*, Op. 19 (1868), and in *Lullaby*, Op. 28, No. 1 (1872). His harmony, however, is stereotyped and unoriginal.

The songs of Samuel P. Warren are among the most musicianly of his time. They show strong Schumann influence, and the craftsmanship is always excel‌‌‌‌‌‌ ‌. Like Brahms, he is fond of allowing voice and piano parts to ‌‌‌‌‌ in thirds and sixths. *The Sea Hath Its Pearls* (1865) is of ‌‌‌‌ texture, with much use of ninth harmonies and sequence. In the two songs from Tennyson (1866), *Miller's Daughter* and *Love That Hath Us in the Net*, the evidence of Warren's admiration for Schumann's style is very marked, resulting, in the case of the second song, in a very attractive and unusual piece of work, which, taken as pure music, still appeals to us of today, though there is no hint of any actual interpretation of the mood of the text. Probably any words could be substituted for those used, with no noticeable loss of unity. *Sea Foam* (1868) is better in this respect, as there persists throughout the song an appropriate surging figure in the accompaniment, for its time a highly distinctive feature. (See Ex. 42 and 43.)

(42) Andante espressivo

Love that Hath Us in the Net—Warren

Love that hath us in___ the net

Can he pass and we___ for - get?

In *Adrian's Apostrophe* (1871) we again glimpse Schumann. In *I Love My Love* (1877), first of *Three Songs,* text by Charles Mackay, we find the first use of mediant modulation in Warren's songs.  *Waiting* (J. Burroughs), 1900, is elaborate, dramatic; *Faithful* (Arthur Grissom), clean cut and skilfully written.

George L. Osgood makes use of imitation between voice and piano in *Flower May Hide Its Lovely Face* (1874), and of sequence in *She Wears a Rose in Her Hair* (1874) and in the waltz song, *Brown Eyes Has That Little Maiden* (1875).  *In May My Dream Came True* (Nathan Haskell Dole), 1898, shows use of mediant modulation. *The Night Has a Thousand Eyes* (1900) is dignified and sincere, and *April, Laugh Thy Girlish Laughter* (William Watson), 1904, is buoyant and interesting, with an effective bit of coloratura at its close.

Sea Foam—Warren

Sing now up-on the si - lent shore, The sad - dest of__ thy songs, oh_ Sea! And

The songs of Henshaw Dana show the ear-marks of romanticism in the use of mediant modulations and sequence; as in *It Was a Knight of Aragon* (T. B. Aldrich) and *Beside the Summer Sea* (William Winter), both of 1878.

Of W. W. Gilchrist's *Song of Doubt and a Song of Love* (J. G. Holland), 1884, the former is elaborate—a veritable *scena*—full of dramatic color, with a varied and interesting piano score; the latter is less successful. *Bugle Song* (Tennyson), 1884, makes clever use of horn intervals; *How Many Thoughts* (1885) shows an excellent recitative-like introduction; *Heart's Delight* (1886), a climax of fine breadth and dramatic value, virile and strong. *Nature's Lullaby* (1893) reminds one of Warren in its Schumannesque texture; *Joys of Spring* (1896) is a brilliant concert song, effective, though not

Nature's Lullaby — Gilchrist

strikingly original, and less good of its type than Chadwick's *Danza*. *Sweet Is True Love* (Tennyson), 1902, is interesting, but, like many of Gilchrist's songs, is of instrumental rather than vocal character. Of Gilchrist's numerous sacred songs the best is *Oh, Lord, Thou Hast Searched Me Out* (1906)—a very musicianly and effective setting of Psalm 139. If one admit the legitimacy of dramatic effects in sacred music, this is one of the very best of American sacred songs.

Silas Gamaliel Pratt was evidently somewhat of the type of "Father" Heinrich in that his ideas were often too big for his utterance. He wrote symphonies and operas, and what is more, they were produced—an orchestral composition of his being given at a regular symphony concert in Berlin. But no one who studies his songs can fail to understand why these larger works were not more successful. *O Holy Night* (*I heard the trailing garments of the night*), Longfellow (1883), is typical. It is partly recitative, dramatically treated—a finely laid out song. It is richly harmonized, and the declamatory portions alternate with sustained cavatina in attractive fashion. But here, too, the technique is far from adequate to the conception. In general, Pratt's songs show lack of discipline, finesse; they are restless, at times awkward. There is unquestioned feeling for color, however, reminding one somewhat of Pease. Was there something about their common teacher, Wuerst, at Leipsic, that gave them both this same characteristic? Or was it inborn?

There is much of refined feeling for harmonic color in W. J. McCoy's *There Are So Many Ways to Love*, Op. 47, No. 1 (Arthur Grissom), 1900; attractive melodic line and tenuous accompaniment in *The Only Voice*, Op. 51, No. 1 (Oscar Weil), 1905; while *In the Shadow of Your Eyes* (Arthur Marvel), 1917, shows attractive texture in its piano score.

In *Daffodils* (1887) Jules Jordan makes curious and interesting use of a trumpet motif, puzzling until the line is reached.

"With golden trumpets in their hands." This anticipatory effect is both original and happy.

*Stay By and Sing* (1888) shows lyric grace, and *Down By the Brook in May Time* (1891) attractive coloratura phrases. In *Triumphant Love* (Kipling), 1892, Jordan attempted the grandiose, and not without a certain dignity and virility, quite

(45)                          Daffodils—Jordan

The songs of Horace Wadham Nicholl, born in England 1848, coming to America 1871, are restless in every sense, harmonically, melodically, rhythmically; and this lack of repose is their chief defect. *Love On* (1876) is interesting for its chorallike melody in its middle section. *I Ask Not* (1876) passes through seven different tonalities in the course of six measures! *Mein Lieb und Ich* (1889), while skilful in its workmanship, shows this same energetic, impetuous, restive character.

For the most part all these writers of songs were also practical musicians: Dudley Buck, organist and writer of church music—the latter field also occupied with distinction by W. W. Gilchrist; George L. Osgood, Clara K. Rogers, and Jules Jordan, singers; S. P. Warren, organist. It would be an interesting study to attempt to determine how far these activities are reflected in their songs.

# CHAPTER VIII

## 1880-1900

*Arthur Foote, George W. Chadwick, Edward MacDowell,*
*James H. Rogers, Ethelbert Nevin, William Arms Fisher,*
*Ernest R. Kroeger, Henry Holden Huss, Horatio Parker,*
*Sidney Homer, Harvey Worthington Loomis,*
*Mrs. H. H. A. Beach, Henry F. Gilbert*

IF we owe to Buck and Bartlett and their contemporaries the establishment upon a permanent basis of the art-song in America, it is to two men of the succeeding decade that we owe its marked development along artistic lines. We recall the suggestions of appropriate and effective writing in some of Francis Hopkinson's songs, the memorable opening phrase of Benjamin Carr's *Ave Maria*, the very real lyric charm in portions of J. C. D. Parker's *Come into the Garden, Maud,* the sumptuous tonal effects of Alfred Pease and Homer Bartlett, the rhythmic vigor of Dudley Buck, and we realize that somehow through the years, the thin, wavering line of American song has gained in strength and firmness until now at the hands of Arthur Foote and George W. Chadwick it may worthily weave itself into the varied pattern of contemporary music. It is to the personality and musicianship of these two men that we owe the giving to our native song a status comparable with that of other lands and times. True, inspiration may sometimes seem to lag in the songs of both these men, but crude they never are nor insincere. Admirable alike in spirit and workmanship, these songs have served as a firm foundation on which to build; and how-

evermuch our present-day song or that of the future may differ
from these in type and style, we shall always look back to them
as the beginning of real artistry in American song.   And it is
an interesting fact that with these men we enter upon our own
contemporary stage; for happily they are both still with us and
still writing songs, the present link that binds us to that past—
neither too remote in time nor, let us hope, in interest—which
we have been considering in these pages.

We may consider, then, that the Present of American song
begins with Arthur Foote (1853-) and George W. Chadwick
(1854-).   Is it not truly a remarkable thing that today, in
1930, it is still possible for us to treat as contemporary, writers
who were also contemporary with the essential beginnings of our
song—contradictory as that may sound?   Yet when we consider
that the whole world was as recently as 1928 celebrating the
centenary of the death of that great originator of song as we
know it today, Franz Schubert, we need not be surprised that our
own recognized efforts along this line fall within the last half-
century.   In a certain sense, perhaps, we may say that our Past
is our Present—that both stages are comprehended in the lives
of these two men.   For not only is it true that American art-
song (if we place the emphasis upon art) takes its real beginning with them, but it is no less true that they have kept pace
with it even up to the very present.   To Foote and Chadwick,
therefore, let us never fail to do grateful homage for their constantly enlarging endeavor in this field.

In Foote's early songs, such as *I'm Wearing Awa' to the
Land o' the Leal* (Lady Nairn), 1887, *In Picardie* (Graham
R. Tomson), 1896, and *A Ditty* (Sir Philip Sidney), 1892, we
find the same singleness of purpose, the same serious, capable
workmanship that we see in his songs of today.   *A Ditty* catches
the very mood of its text—there is the same light, delicate touch;
while in *In Picardie* the deliberate movement, the expressive

(47)   Allegretto grazioso                               A Ditty——Foote

My   true-love hath  my   heart, and - I have
his, By   just ex-change one  to  the oth-er   given:——

intervals, are equally potent in interpreting the meditative mood
of the verses.   And so it is with his later songs; *A Twilight Fear*
(C. G. Blanden), 1918, is simplicity itself.   I commend it to
our young writers as a model of expressive brevity, of artistic
restraint.   Of like simplicity is *The Red Rose Whispers
Passion* (John Boyle O'Reilly), 1919.   We may well note the
unaffected eloquence of the phrase "And the white rose is a
dove."   Always sensitive to harmonic color, although at times
in a peculiarly dispassionate way, in which he somewhat re-
sembles MacDowell, Foote has continually grown with the years.
His later songs show much more individuality and imaginative
treatment than those of earlier date, as witness the constantly
shifting color of *Tranquillity* (Mary van Orden), 1915, the strikingly Brahmsian middle section of *Lilac Time* (Alfred Noyes),

1917, the lyric fluency of *How Many Times Do I Love Thee, Dear* (Thomas Lovell Beddoes), 1919, and the atmospheric final cadences of both *A Twilight Fear* and *Ships That Pass in the Night* (Longfellow), 1921;

Ships that pass in the Night——Foote

gain,— and a    si - lence.

and I doubt if anything more genuine in a musical way came
out of the war than Foote's simple, sincere, heartfelt set of *Three
Songs*, Op. 79—*In Flanders' Fields* (Lieut.-Col. John McCrae),
*The Soldier* (Rupert Brooke), *Oh, Red is the English Rose* (Dr.
Charles Alexander Richmond).

With a richer palette than Foote's, a more decorative use
of contrapuntal devices in his piano score, and more suavity
of style, but certainly with no more unerring instinct for that
which is artistically appropriate, Chadwick's songs filled a large
place in our national song consciousness for many decades.    His
early setting of Heine's much set verses *Du bist wie eine
Blume*, 1883, is fluent and graceful, not without very real
charm, *Allah* (Longfellow), 1887, is characterized by a simple
dignity of utterance, and *The Danza* (Arlo Bates), 1885, has
distinct refinement, with interesting contrapuntal variety in the
midst of its gay dance rhythms.    *A Ballad of Trees and the
Master*, 1899, is serious and deeply felt, even though it seems
scarcely to do justice to the infinite pathos of Sidney Lanier's
verses.    The much-sung *Bedouin Love Song* (Bayard Taylor),
1890, has characteristic vigor and verve, and its long-drawn-out
final climax is developed with true dramatic instinct.    From
*Told in the Gate* (1897), a collection of eleven songs to poems
by Arlo Bates, *Sweetheart, Thy Lips Are Touched with Flame*

and *Oh, Let Night Speak of Me* are particularly successful, the former through the appropriate intensity of its expression, the latter by reason of its sincerity and depth of feeling.

Sweetheart, thy lips are touched with flame — Chadwick

(49)  Molto appassionato

Sweet - heart, thy lips are touched with flame;

Sweet - heart, thy glow - ing ar - dor tame; Sweet-

heart\_\_\_\_\_ thy love how can I blame, When

I \_\_\_\_\_ too, feel its fire,\_\_\_\_\_ When

Copyright, 1897, by Arthur P. Schmidt.

Oh, let night speak of me—Chadwick

(50) Molto moderato

Oh, let night speak of me,\_\_\_\_\_

for day Knows not how breaks with woe    my heart;

Day knows not how   I mourn-ful stray,   Weep-ing for

thee,      so dear thou   art.

Copyright, 1897, by Arthur P. Schmidt.

In *When I Am Dead* (Christina Rossetti), 1910, our composer
gives expression to a pathos unusual in his songs; while Tempo
di Bolero in *The Daughter of Mendoza* (M. B. Lamar), 1914,
is most ingratiating.   Chadwick has done little song-writing of
late years, the most recent things to come to my notice being the

rollicking set of *Three Nautical Songs*: *The Admirals* (R. D. Ware), *Drake's Drum* (Henry Newbolt), and *Pirate Song* (Conan Doyle), 1920.

Following upon Foote's and Chadwick's earlier works, come songs by James H. Rogers (1857-), Edward MacDowell (1861-1908), Ethelbert Nevin (1862-1901), William Arms Fisher (1861-), Ernest R. Kroeger (1862-), Henry Holden Huss (1862-), Horatio Parker (1863-1920), Sidney Homer (1864-), Harvey Worthington Loomis (1865-), Mrs. H. H. A. Beach (1867-), Henry F. Gilbert (1868-1928) and others, fortunately most of them still actively writing.

James H. Rogers' most important songs come almost within the last decade, including the two cycles *Five Quatrains from Omar Khayyám* and *In Memoriam*, and such admirable songs as *The Time for Making Songs Has Come* (Hermann Hagedorn) and *The Last Song* (Hartley Alexander).

Of the songs of Edward MacDowell it is scarcely necessary at this time to speak. Henry T. Finck to the contrary notwithstanding (though one hesitates to disagree with so distinguished an authority on songs and song-writers), I cannot feel that MacDowell's songs, taken as a whole, are particularly distinctive. His medium was primarily the piano. Are the *Four Songs*, Op. 56, to be compared for one moment with the *Woodland Sketches*, Op. 51, or the *Sea Pieces*, Op. 55? Is there among all his songs a melody as fragrant as that of the *Wild Rose?*

If we take his songs *seriatim*, it is curious to see in what respects his technical style changed between the *Five Songs*, Op. 11 and 12, and *Four Songs*, Op. 56, from a full, opulent piano score to the barest chords, followed in Op. 58 and 60 by a partial return to the earlier manner. Apparently MacDowell felt the very great danger—ever present in song writing—of submerging the voice in a heavy sea of externality, and very soon began cutting his piano score down to the merest background for the vocal line.  One can not help the feeling, however, that he was altogether too rigorous in this process.  If rather he had kept somewhat more to the technique of his earlier songs, giving them the added richness and power of his maturing ability, as he very patently began to do in the *Three Songs*, Op. 60, his songs as a whole would have gained immeasurably. As it is, the earlier songs have a certain attractiveness that many of the later ones lack.  It is unfortunate, too, that MacDowell treated the voice part with such persistent metrical regularity. This habit grew upon him, it is true, but it was present even in his earlier songs.  If only he could have treated the vocal line with greater freedom, it would have added much of spontaneity, of fluency, and dramatic value to his songs.  This unvaried metrical persistence in the voice part, coupled with complete lack of contrasting melodies, of counter rhythms in piano score, often places the undeniable artistry of MacDowell under too heavy a handicap in his songs.

The early songs, *Mein Liebchen*,        11, No. 1, and *Nachtlied*, Op. 12, No. 1, are fairly Strauss     ia the freedom of the counter melodies in the piano score, in th.     uty of the modulations.  *Oben wo die Sterne glühen*, Op. 1  No. 3 (Heine), is quite unusual among MacDowell's songs for the contrast between the rhythms of voice and piano.  There is a certain breadth, dignity—even solemnity—of movement in this song that is very satisfying.  *From an Old Garden, Six Songs* (Margaret Deland), Op. 26 (1887), abounds in deft poetic touches, as at the words "a bit of heaven" in *The Myrtle* and "he flew away" in *The Bluebell*, while the characterization of the *Sturdy Clover* is altogether delightful.  *Idyll*, Op. 33, No. 3 (Goethe), is rendered distinctive by the dainty staccato accompaniment of the piano against a sustained long-breathed cantilena of the voice, with the welcome alternation of $\frac{2}{4}$ and $\frac{3}{4}$ rhythm. In *Six Songs*, Op. 40 (W. H. Gardner), 1890, we catch certain glimpses of the earlier freedom of style.   In the first song, *Sweet Blue-Eyed Maid*, the accompaniment is quite individualized, even the regularity of the voice part broken at times; in *Sweetheart, Tell Me* there is a most charming obbligato melody in the accompaniment; *Thy Beaming Eyes*, however, shows but two measures in which the accompaniment does not follow the voice, note for note; *For Sweet Love's Sake*, excellent as it is as music, might take to itself any words whatsoever, or no words at all, and remain equally attractive.   *Oh, Lovely Rose* and *I Ask but This* are interesting bits of lyricism, the latter with an accompaniment buoyant enough in itself, but the vocal line again absolutely uninterrupted.   In *Eight Songs*, Op. 47, we find two of MacDowell's best known songs, the inimitable *Midsummer Lullaby*, (after Goethe), where what is a defect in most songs becomes a real advantage, and the uninterrupted, persistent movement of his shimmering harmonies produces just the right dreamy effect, an absolutely perfect fusion of the idea and its expression, and *The Sea* (Howells), which, while very attractive in its rich harmonic coloring, quite fails to express in its vocal line the tragic drama of the text.   *Long Ago* (the first of *Four Songs*, Op. 56), 1898, has a rich, expressive melodic line, but un-

Midsummer Lullaby—MacDowell

Sil - ver clouds are light - ly sail - ing

Through the drow - sy, trem-bling air, And the gold - en

*slightly retard*

sum - mer sun - shine Casts a glo - ry ev - 'ry-where.

*retard*

Permission by Asso Music Inc., N.Y.C.

questionably the most successful song in this group is the buoyant
and lilting *A Maid Sings Light and a Maid Sings Low*, surely
one of MacDowell's best songs.   Here is no suggestion of dull
perfunctoriness, but rather the utmost buoyancy and lightness of
touch.   Beginning with *Three Songs*, Op. 58 (1899), and continuing through *Three Songs*, Op. 60 (1902), there is a decided
growth in imaginative treatment, in fluency of expression.   *Sunrise*, from Op. 58, contains some of MacDowell's best lines; while
*Merry Maiden Spring* is a fit companion to *A Maid Sings Light
and a Maid sings Low*.   In the last group of MacDowell's published songs, *Three Songs*, Op. 60, we find what seems to be the
most consistently developed group in all his songs.   The quaintly
archaic character of *Tyrant Love* is most delightfully reflected in

the music and with unwonted rhythmic freedom.  The passage
beginning "Yet though the tears be bitter-sweet" from *Fair
Springtide,*

Fair Springtide—MacDowell

Copyright, 1902, by Arthur P. Schmidt.

and similarly effective parts of *To a Golden Rod* point clearly
to his earlier freer style, and seem to imply that MacDowell's
best songs were never written.  Indeed, we have every reason
to believe that if he had lived, his later songs would have shown
an ever-increasing freedom of treatment, an ever-growing beauty
of expression.

Probably no review of American song during these decades
could be considered in any sense complete that left out of

account the songs of Ethelbert Nevin, which enjoyed such
tremendous vogue in their time.   Nor was this entirely a mis-
taken enthusiasm; for while Nevin possessed no profundity of musical thought, he did have to a marked degree a feeling for fluent
melody, a limited but expressive (though unfortunately often
oversentimentalized) harmonic sense, and a certain buoyancy of
style not at all to be despised.   The almost maudlin *Oh! that
we two were Maying* (Kingsley) is at once, probably, his most
familiar and his worst song, and yet even here his handling of
"O'er river, and mead, and town," is distinctly not unimpressive.

William Arms Fisher delights in a rich, sonorous harmonization which he utilizes with fine effect in *The Singer's Wish*
(Sara Teasdale), 1921.  Very attractive is the pictorial touch

(53)                              Oh that we two were Maying—Nevin

limbs    at rest    on    the    qui - et earth's breast, And our

souls___ at home_____ with

at the words "falling star." *I Wait for Thee* (Arthur T. Frog-
gatt), first issued in 1893 and reissued in revised form in 1920,
is characterized by the same richness of harmonic texture, while
*As Once in May* (von Gilm) is a sterling song worthy to be
ranked with the best settings of this well-known text. Special
mention must also be made of Fisher's unusually skilful arrangement of numerous Irish songs and Negro Spirituals.

Ernest R. Kroeger has written many well-known songs, as
have Henry Holden Huss and Sidney Homer. Kroeger's suave
and lovely *Bend Low, O Dusky Night*, 1911, remains unmatched
among his songs, we might almost say among all contemporary
songs, in its absolute simplicity and velvet-like smoothness of
texture. His *Love's Power* (Elizabeth K. Reynolds), 1911, is

(54) *più mosso*

The Singer's wish — Fisher

If I could make— a sin-gle song As love-ly and as full of light,— As hush'd and brief as a fall— —ing— star,

On a win-ter night,

an ingenious and finely wrought example of interdependence of voice and piano, while *Above the Stars* (text by the composer), 1916, is perhaps the most deeply felt and atmospheric of his songs.

We wish that Henry Holden Huss could be induced to write more songs of the type of his *It Was a Lover and His Lass*, 1907. To us it is the best song he has written. In it he has caught exactly the right quaint and archaic style, and a very attractive style it is. There is just enough harmonic variety, neither too much nor too little, and the unexpected turn that he gives the winsome melody of his opening bars when it recurs between the verses, is exceedingly whimsical and attractive.

Love's Power---Kroeger

(55)  Lento e rubato

He whom thine eyes have

cantando ed espressivo

His setting of the Burns poem *While Larks With Little Wing*, 1910, would be equally effective and from a harmonic standpoint even more so, were it not that unfortunately it lacks the unity and directness of the other. Perhaps the most imaginative song that Huss has written is *Before Sunrise* (R. W. Gilder), 1907.

It was a lover and his lass — Huss

It was a lov-er and his lass, With a
hey, and a ho, and a hey non-i-no, That
o'er the green corn-field did pass, In the

spring-time,    the on - ly pret - ty    ring - time,     When

Here we find the harmonic scheme richer and more expressive, the rhythm more flexible than in many of his songs.

With all his song writing, it is doubtful if Sidney Homer has ever written anything more telling than his early *Sing Me a*

(57) Allegro *Spirited*   f      Sing me a song of a lad that is gone — Homer

Sing   me a song   of a    lad    that is gone,

Say, could that lad   be    I?      Mer - ry of soul   he__

sailed on a day    O - ver the sea    to Skye

*Song of a Lad that is Gone* (R. L. Stevenson), 1904, a song redolent of the sea and the sky, and whose rollicking style is delightfully characteristic.

Horatio W. Parker's songs may sometimes lack spontaneity, but are always written with great skill and much harmonic richness. Perhaps no American song-writer of his time surpasses him in freedom and variety of the piano score. It is always entirely independent of the voice, and abounds in free obbligato melodies of great effectiveness. His early song, *Pack Clouds Away* (Thomas Heywood), 1891, is not only rich in color, but fluent in its movement—a condition not always present in these songs. *I Know a Little Rose*, Op. 34, No. 1 (1893), is of unusually simple, harmonic construction, but of very real lyric charm. Of his *Four Songs*, Op. 59 (1904), *Serenade* (Nathan Haskell Dole) is attractive in its thin, open texture, while *Good Bye* (Christina Rossetti) is of a sombre color, unusual with Parker. *Crépuscule*, Op. 64 (J. DeBeaufort), 1912, is an elaborate and richly scored aria. *In a Garden* (Brian Hooker), from the opera *Fairyland* (1915), is a really distinctive song, almost austere in its harmonization, but as graceful and tenuous in its texture as the earlier songs had been rich and full.

In a Garden—Parker

(58)

In a gar-den glad and green   Blooms a rose,   un-known,   un- seen,   Ru-by- bo-somed like a flame, Ho-ly like a ho - ly name,

*colla voce*

Perhaps the best known—and deservedly so—of Parker's songs is *The Lark Now Leaves His Watery Nest*, from *Six Old English Songs*, Op. 47 (1899). Its thoroughly objective character is peculiarly congenial to Parker's style, and the result is a song quite perfect of its type.

The delicacy and grace that Harvey Worthington Loomis knows so well how to impart to his writing, so particularly appropriate to the setting of child's verse, is well exemplified in *A Little Dutch Garden* (Hattie Whitney), 1910. We see the more serious side of his musical personality in the brief but poignant *Epitaph upon a Virgin* (Robert Herrick), 1902; while the strong individuality of Henry F. Gilbert finds expression in songs like *The Croon of the Dew* (George Turner Phelps), 1914, and *Bring from the craggy haunts of birch and pine* (John Todhunter), from *Celtic Studies*, 1909.

Mrs. H. H. A. Beach has never given us finer work than in her setting of Robert Browning's *Ah, Love, but a Day*, a truly distinctive song in its sincerity and depth of feeling, the close being particularly effective in its clever psychological development, its wistfulness and pathos.

Ah, Love, but a day!—Beach

eyes,_____ Look in my eyes,_____

Wilt thou change too?_____

Equally attractive in altogether different manner is its companion piece, *The Year's at the Spring,* issued in the same year, 1904. In 1924 Mrs. Beach published two songs with violin and 'cello, *The Mirage* (Bertha Ochsner) and *Stella Viatoris* (Jessie H. Nettleton), and in 1928, *Rendezvous* (Leonora Speyer) also with violin, all written with her accustomed skill. The last named song is particularly distinguished for its freshness and spontaneity.

Among others who during this period have helped either

(60) Allegro di molto

The Year's at the Spring——Beach

The year's__ at the spring,_____ And day's__ at the

morn;_____ Morn - ing's at sev - en; The

hill side's dew - pearled;_____

qualitatively or quantitatively—happily oftentimes both—to establish American song as it stands today are the following well-known writers. Obviously, however, it is impossible either to make such a list complete or to go into any detail; the most that

can be done is to note here and there a certain few representative
songs, generally of fairly recent date:

A. M. Foerster, 1854-1927
    *A Wreath of Songs,* Op. 70, 1910

Wilson G. Smith, 1855-1929

Mary Turner Salter, 1856
    *The Cry of Rachel* (Lizette Woodworth Reese), 1905
    Two Songs: *The Moth, We Two* (Patience Worth), 1920

J. H. Brewer, 1856

Helen Hopekirk, 1856

Clayton Johns, 1857

Edgar Stillman Kelley, 1857
    *Eldorado* (Poe)
    *Israfel* (Poe), 1901

Henry Schoenefeld, 1857

Mary Knight Wood, 1857

Frank Lynes, 1858-1913

Harry Rowe Shelley, 1858

Frank Van der Stucken, 1858-1929
    *Waldesrauschen* (Paul Remer), 1910

B. O. Klein, 1858-1911
    *Four Songs,* Op. 89, 1907

Reginald De Koven, 1859-1920

Whitney Coombs, 1859

Gerrit Smith, 1859-1912
    Cycle—*Thistledown* (Cora Fabbri), 1907

Homer Norris, 1860-1920
    *Four Songs,* 1900

Arthur B. Whiting, 1861
    *Three Songs* (Christina Rossetti), Op. 18, 1904

R. Huntington Woodman, 1861
    *In the Night* (Elizabeth E. Moore), 1923

Carl Busch, 1862

EUGENE MURDOCK, 1862
*My True Love Lies Asleep* (Lizette Woodworth Reese), 1919

HELEN HOOD, 1863

W. H. NEIDLINGER, 1863-1924

ELEANOR EVEREST FREER, 1864

FREDERICK FIELD BULLARD, 1864-1904
*Six Songs,* Op. 14, 1893

BENJAMIN WHELPLEY, 1864

HARRY T. BURLEIGH, 1866
*The Sailor's Wife* (Mary S. Cutting), 1917

ROSSETER G. COLE, 1866
*Three Songs,* Op. 37, 1922

FLORENCE NEWELL BARBOUR, 1867
*O Wild West Wind* (Shelley), 1922
*Tell Me, Thou Wanderer* (Shelley), 1923

MARGARET RUTHVEN LANG, 1867
*Album of Ten Songs*

CHARLES S. SKILTON, 1868
*Departure* (Hermann Hagedorn), 1925
*The Sea Lands* (Orrick Johns), 1925

LOUIS VICTOR SAAR, 1868
*Four Seasons* (John Murray Gibbon), 1927 (A Canadian Song Cycle)

SAMUEL RICHARDS GAINES, 1869

W. V. HARRIS, 1869
*Nod* ⎫
*Silver* ⎬ (Walter de la Mare), 1921

# CHAPTER IX

## 1900-1930

*Ernest Bloch, Charles M. Loeffler, George F. Boyle,*
*Marion Bauer, Frederick Jacobi, Emerson Whithorne,*
*Arthur Shepherd, Carl Engel, John Beach, Oscar G. Sonneck,*
*Alexander Steinert, Jr., Frederic Ayres, Arthur Farwell,*
*Howard Brockway, Alexander Rihm, Henry Hadley,*
*David Stanley Smith, Richard Hageman, Charles Fonteyn*
*Manney, John Powell, Carl Deis, Edward Ballantine,*
*George Harris*

AS the world at large has its Stravinsky, its Schönberg, its Milhaud, so we in American song have our own modernist group, not so large perhaps as one might expect, but vigorous and flourishing.

There may well be good and sufficient reasons for the fact that our most pronounced modernists are not so much our own native-born Americans as those who have come to us from other lands. Certain it is that no one now resident in America seems to have done more convincing work along these ultramodern lines than the Swiss-born Ernest Bloch (1880-). His work is always characterized by the utmost skill in craftsmanship, and while no one could ever accuse him of any reticence in individual self-expression, he is never guilty of incoherence or formlessness. Rather there is a fine sense of logic, of unity and symmetry in all that he does; a firmness of substance that can come only from keen thinking. And in a feeling for what is sombre, stern, tragic, in musical expression he is probably unsurpassed today.

As to his songs, no one can study his earlier *Poèmes d'* *Automne* (Béatrix Rodès), 1918, without being moved by their pathos, and feeling a deep admiration for the personality able to evoke such intensely human moods as these.    This admiration for Bloch as a transcriber of the deeper human emotions is only strengthened by his powerful *Psalms 114 and 137*, and that great dramatic monologue, *Psalm 22*, all of 1919, where he not only searches the soul's deepest depths, but in the final climax rises to superb heights of spiritual ecstasy.    It is powerful writing—that of a hand sure of its own strength.

Charles M. Loeffler (1861-), while writing with the same genuineness and, too, with a full rich texture of his own, apparently avoids the deeply tragic and deals preferably with themes of less passionate utterance, yet with no less sincerity of expression.    In his songs, at any rate, Loeffler shows more the Debussy influence; but he is far from being a mere imitator: his own artistic personality is too vigorous for that.

His latest songs as far as I know them, *The Wind Among the Reeds* (W. B. Yeats), published in 1908—it seems incredible that there should be no songs of more recent date than these—are delightfully imaginative, and expressed with all the charm of style that we have come to expect from him.    Perhaps, however, he never wrote a song of more tender beauty, of more expressive simplicity (for expressiveness may be simple!), than his earlier song *To Helen* (Edgar Allan Poe), 1906.

(61)    *dolce*                                          To Helen—Loeffler

Hel- en,    thy beau - ty is to    me    Like those Ni-cé-an

barks    of yore,    That gen-tly, o'er a per-fumed sea,    The

wear-y, way-worn wan-derer bore    To his own na-tive

shore.

Still unlike either our Swiss or French co-workers, is he from Australia, George F. Boyle (1886-), but with a skill in expression quite his own. Boyle's songs are very happy in their successful delineation of utterly diverse moods. *A Spirit Haunts the Year's Last Hours* (Tennyson), 1922, is, of course, dull grey throughout, and the sombre color of the text is reproduced in the music with extraordinary fidelity; but so ably done, and with such musicianship, that there is no monotony of effect. In *Proud Maisie*, Boyle gives us an extremely interesting treatment of Sir Walter Scott's fantastic verses. One is tempted to dwell on his clever use of cross rhythms, of dark and gloomy harmonization of the simplest melody, all serving to accentuate the sinister portent of the words. One technical point is much in evidence—almost a mannerism, in fact. What the subdominant color is to Wintter Watts, such is the verbatim repetition in the accompaniment of a closing phrase in the voice part, to Boyle. He uses it time and again in all his songs. But here so clearly do these short, reiterated phrases seem to reinforce the mood that is past or anticipate the mood that is to come, that they become a very important element in his interpretational mechanism. Eugene Field's exquisite *Little Blue Pigeon* receives equally sympathetic and attractive setting, while *Breath of Roses* (Strickland Galli-lan) is a bit of pure lyricism. All these songs are of 1922.

Of our own American-born members of this modernist group, first place should be given to Charles T. Griffes (1884-1920). I know of nothing in this field finer than his *Three Poems* by Fiona MacLeod (*Lament of Ian the Proud, Thy Dark Eyes to Mine, The Rose of the Night*), 1918, and *In a Myrtle Shade* (William Blake) and *Wai Kiki* (Rupert Brooks), also 1918, with the possible addition of the *Two Poems* by John Masefield— *An Old Song Resung* and *Sorrow of Mydath*—issued posthumously, 1920. In all of Griffes' work there is present the same sense of logical development, of artistic sincerity, that we see in the case of Ernest Bloch. In fact it would seem that there is more than a superficial kinship between their artistic natures.

With the opening section of Marion Bauer's *Roses Breathe*

*in the Night* (Margaret Widdemer), published in 1921, it seemed quite evident that the composer was beginning to find her true self.  Her means of obtaining a remarkably attractive atmospheric effect were simple but unusual, reminding one of a similarly clever device in Duparc's *Chanson Triste*.  This growing power of self-expression has fully flowered in *Four Poems*, Op. 16, to texts by John Gould Fletcher, 1924, which form a notable contribution to American Song.  Here, once more, we see it made perfectly clear that the freest possible use of modern color and effect is entirely compatible with an underlying sense of form and a very real appreciation of the value of an expressive melodic line, as we have already seen it so abundantly proved in the songs of Griffes.  Indeed, in easy command of modern technique, in rich pictorial quality, in vivid play of the imagination and sustained dramatic interest, these songs may worthily take their place beside Griffes' own.

Frederick Jacobi (1891-) has written few songs, but their quality is in an inverse ratio to their quantity.  His two songs to texts by Chaucer, *Rondel* and *Ballade* (1923), are the work of a thoroughgoing musician, written in the quaint old-fashioned style absolutely appropriate to their text.  The *Ballade* is particularly vivacious and abounds in telling effects.  Ever since it was issued in 1918, *The Faery Isle of Janjira* (Sarojini Naidu) has been one of my most treasured songs, notable for the aristocratic elegance of its rhythms and deft melodic touches. *In the Night*, from the same set of three songs to texts by the same author, is only second in interest and attractiveness, and the remaining *Love and Death* is a dramatic song of great emotional power.

I have never been quite able to grasp why the Orient should seem to possess such an overwhelming appeal for our songwriters.  One can understand the attractiveness of writing in an idealized oriental atmosphere, as Carpenter has done in

*Water Colors;* there it is a matter of tone-color, but still attractive and comprehensive to Western ears. But when Emerson Whithorne (1884-) writes almost exclusively to Chinese texts, and chooses not to mitigate what seems to us the uncouthness of either rhythm, melody, or harmonic background, he is of course entirely within his rights, but it certainly cannot fail to diminish his audience materially, for to most of us a very little of anything so entirely foreign to our own idiom suffices. For this reason I can admire all the cleverness and ingenuity he puts into these songs—from a distance! It is only when he comes to a text like Walt Whitman's *Invocation* (1921), that I feel able to meet him on common ground. This is a massive and powerful song; and while there are moments in which the harmonization seems unnecessarily vague and obscure, still the song is laid out with great skill and effectiveness. The *marche funèbre* motif at the beginning and the end is both impressive and touching, while the final climax is of great dramatic vigor. In very different mood is *Pierrette and I* (Hugh McCrae), 1922, a slight bit of fantasy, but wonderfully attractive in its deliciously acrid harmonization. Unusually suave for Whithorne, in its general outline, is his setting of Eugene Field's *The Babe in the Garden* (1917). The finest thing that has come from his hand, however, is the recent *The Grim Troubadour*, Op. 45 (Countee Cullen), for voice and string quartet (1927). Here, along with most modern feeling for subtle harmonic color, interesting rhythms, and the like, we yet find an expressive vocal line, exquisitely molded, to conform to every *nuance* of the text; the whole song (there are three sections) convincing in every detail —an artistic and beautiful piece of work.

Excellent use of voice and strings is also made in Arthur Shepherd's (1880-) *Triptych* for High Voice and String Quartet (1927), text by Tagore. The three movements are admirably individualized and interestingly portrayed. It is

thoughtful, sincere, musicianly music.    Shepherd also published
in the Wa-Wan Press—that interesting American nationalistic
experiment of the early twentieth century—*Five Songs*, Op. 7
(1907), poems by Lowell, of which *There is a Light in Thy Blue
Eyes* and *The Lost Child* are particularly to be mentioned, the
former for the buoyancy of its mood, the latter, the richness of
its texture.    The composer's sense of natural and spontaneous
declamation stands him in good stead in all these songs.

Another attraction seemingly very potent these days is
toward the setting of free verse, and the freest of free verse at
that.    We find an interesting case of this in Carl Engel's three
Amy Lowell songs, *Opal*, *A Decade* and *A Sprig of Rosemary*
(1922).    These settings are as truly imagist as the verses themselves.    There is much of the later Scriabin about them, the
same rhythmic vitality, the same intellectuality (there is no loose
thinking here, as in so much of the ultramodernist writing of
today), even a similar tonal scheme.

*Opal* is lurid, volcanic, brusque, with a powerful and compelling harmonization.    But is it a song?    Or is *A Decade*?
I would give a very great deal to hear this latter in orchestral
dress, with the oboe taking the melody instead of the voice.    It
would make a most pathetic and expressive intermezzo in the
midst of some stormy orchestral tone poem.    But is there any
conceivable connection between its mood expression and that of
"morning bread," "red wine and honey"?    On the other hand,
*A Sprig of Rosemary* is in very truth a song, to my mind the
only one of the three.    They are all instrumentally effective,
but only as absolute music; and except in the case of this one,
seem merely marred by the attaching of words—that too, in
spite of the great expertness with which the declamation is
handled.    Here, however, we are conscious of no lack of cohesion
between the music and the vocal line of the text; they form an
organically unified whole.    We quote the skilfully handled final
cadence:

A Sprig of Rosemary — Engel

And the soft___ bright - ness___ which is your soul.

Interesting as are these three songs in showing Engel's command of manifold resources, they do not compare in general interest, it seems to me, with his *Chansons Intimes* (Jean Moréas), 1910.   In these six songs we find the utmost variety of mood, interpreted with great skill.   Not only has our composer shown himself keenly sensitive to these various moods, but he has had the ability to express them worthily in his music— from the stark ruggedness of *A l'ocean* to the exquisite tender-

ness and grace of *Mer natale*. *En outre*, too, is most sym-
pathetically and attractively done.

Granting, however, that any text whatsoever may be set to
music, and in any way whatsoever, Engel has shown in his
Amy Lowell songs how it may be done with consistency and a
sense of logical procedure. It is this saving grace in his case
which seems to be so woefully lacking in certain other treatments
of similar texts, as for instance the *Free Verse Songs* of Rupert
Hughes (1872-). Here, barring a few measures which show
some signs of rhyme and reason, we have only a mass of conglom-
erate details, with no apparent feeling of unity whatever, no
development, no semblance of logical sequence. Hughes has
shown, however, that his mind does not always and necessa-
rily travel in this zigzag fashion, in such songs as his setting
of Shakespeare's 71st Sonnet under the title *Remember Not*
(1922), which though rather uncouth in its expression, is a
sincere and expressive song. Quite unusually successful is his
rhythmic and tonal treatment of the words "Than you shall hear
the surly, sullen bell."

Two interestingly atmospheric settings in the ultramodern
manner are those of John Beach (1877-) to Carl Sandburg's
*Passers-By* and *Clark Street Bridge* (1923). Whatever may
be our opinion as to the advisability of setting such texts as these
to music, there can be no question as to the musicianliness with
which Beach has done his work. In both songs his harmonic
scheme is logical and interesting. With all its nebulousness in
expressing, as he does, monotony of movement, the distant roar
of the city, mist and the like, there is all the time the sense of an
underlying vigorous organism.

The same and more may be said of his recent setting of two
Oppenheim poems—*Wings* and *The Cup of Dew*, both 1928.
In all these later songs Beach disregards entirely the vocal line
as such. The voice part at times consists of little more than free

declamation, at times rises for a brief moment to true melody;
the purpose clearly being to present in any interesting way the
mood picture of the text, makng use of any appropriate means
to that end—least of all to write a song in the old accepted sense

The Cup of Dew—Beach

Dew of the stars and of the e-ther and earth, Dew_ of my soul, Fall in-to the cup of my be-seech-ing hands, That

really so much greater and deeper and more comprehensive than those of Beethoven, Wagner, Schumann and Brahms, that even in accompanying a simple song we must needs make use of three staves, all of them as full of notes as they may comfortably be?   As far as my own modest judgment goes, I find it difficult to forget the point made in my early training, that a composer's ideas are often in inverse proportion to the number of his notes! Not at all so extreme in any way, and of a far lovelier texture, is Steinert's earlier song, *My Lady of Clouds* (Lillian Gertrude Shuman), 1921.

The later songs of Frederic Ayres (1876-1926), while not ultramodern in any sense whatever, are powerful, impressive songs of a certain masculine ruggedness of style that is very heartening.   The *Three Songs* published in 1921 represent him at his best—*Triumph* (William Vaughn Moody) being one of the most telling songs published in America in recent years.   In the declamation of the text, in its harmonization and general mood expression, it is a big, heroic song (see Ex. 65).   *The Song of the Panthan Girl* (Kipling) is notable for the manner in which the original background is suggested rather than actually presented, which, as I have already stated, is (to my mind, at least) the more artistic method.   The dirge-like rhythms in *Strong as Death* (H. C. Bunner ) are presented with unusual skill.

Among Arthur Farwell's (1872-) songs *The Wild Flower's Song* (1920) is attractive in its simplicity of style, exactly fitting the William Blake text.   This simplicity is retained throughout the song, in spite of the fact that the harmonies are rich and novel.   In this combination of simple feeling and rich harmonic color it is a notable song.   The same also may be said of *On a Faded Violet* (1927), one of his settings of *Three Poems* by Shelley, Op. 43.   Although this later song abounds in the most modern harmonic effects, it nevertheless is able to maintain a studied simplicity, which but adds to the effectiveness of its subtle characterization (see Ex. 66).

(65)                                                        Triumph—Ayres

Of wounds and sore de-feat    I
made my bat - tle stay;    Wing'd san-dals for my
feet    I wove of my de-lay;    Of

On a Faded Violet — Farwell

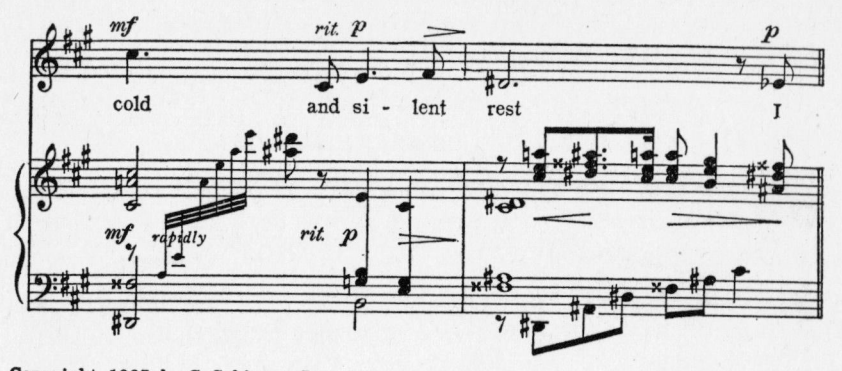

cold          and si - lent  rest              I

*Daughter of Ocean* of the same set of songs shows fine vigor and
sweep. Another recent song of similar spirit, though more
tragically colored, is *Dark Her Lodge Door*, Op. 69, No. 3
(Charles Roos), 1927, in which Farwell makes interesting use
of an Indian motif. Of *Three Dickinson Poems* (1928), *Summer Shower*, Op. 73, No. 1, is appropriately of the daintiest,
most filmy substance, *Mine*, Op. 73, No. 2, an exultant paean,
intense both in color and mood, while *The Sea of Sunset*, Op. 26,
is painted with broad brush, though of a languorous movement,
which well interprets "the western mystery." It is doubtful,
however, if Farwell ever wrote a more powerful song than *The
Ravens are Singing*, Op. 69, No. 1 (Charles O. Roos), 1929.
Here the sombre melody, set against the dirge-like accompaniment with its unceasing, sinister drum-beats, is handled with
great skill. The dark color of the whole, yet with no monotony
of effect, indicates interpretative and technical craftsmanship of
a high order. All of Farwell's recent songs show fine command
of modern harmonization.

Howard Brockway (1870-) has gained an excellent name
for himself through his *Lonesome Tunes* (1916) and *Kentucky
Mountain Songs* (1920), prepared in collaboration with Loraine
Wyman. These are exceedingly interesting arrangements of
unsuspected old English ballads and folk-songs in our very

midst.   Brockway has made the ground quite his own and has done his work with ingenuity and true musicianliness.   Nor should we overlook his unusually attractive song, *An Answer* (Owen Bruner), 1911, the delicate fragility of whose harmonies reminds us not unworthily of MacDowell's *Midsummer Lullaby*.

For a pure lyric gift, expressed always with simplicity but with never-failing grace, we have no composer to surpass Alexander Rihm (1870-).   Of his *Three Songs* published in 1918, *Thou and I* (Sidney Lanier) is a perfectly finished *lied* of the true German type and might without shame be signed by a Schumann himself.   *Her Lullaby* (Lorena Zeller), while of conventional material, is marked by many artistic touches.   The third song, *The Rose* (Sara Teasdale), is utterly charming from its first note to its last, in its fluency of utterance and yet rich musicianship.   One rarely finds a song of such transparent texture and yet no hint of the commonplace.   Rihm's skill in handling contrapuntal melodies is abundantly shown in *To One Away* and *Joy*—both to Sara Teasdale texts—the latter being one of the best settings I know of these popular verses, in the vigor of its themes and their handling.   *Pack, Clouds, Away* (Thomas Heywood) is of appropriately facile technique, and Sara Teasdale's *Wood Song*, while somewhat unoriginal, is characterized by Rihm's unfailing refinement of style (all of 1919).

Henry Hadley's (1871-) songs show the technical dexterity we should expect from him; and of late have disclosed an increasing solidity of workmanship.   His early song *I Plucked a Quill from Cupid's Wing* (Aubrey Boucicault), 1900, will never lose its freshness; and similar in the spontaneity of its expression is the later song, *The Lute-Player of Casa Blanca* (Laurence Hope), 1921.   Of unwonted seriousness and restraint is *Stille, träumende Frühlingsnacht* (Otto Julius Bierbaum), 1911, and *Il pleut des pétales de fleurs* (Alfred Samain), 1909, is a most engaging mood picture.   Mr. Hadley's harmonization of the passage beginning "quelle est donc" is as felicitous as it is un-usual.

But perhaps the very best songs he has yet written are *The Time of Parting* (Tagore), 1921, and *Colloque Sentimentale* (Verlaine), 1923. The latter of course challenges comparison with Debussy's setting of the same text, and while it lacks the eerie quality of the French song (particularly Debussy's organ-point maintained with such uncanny effect throughout the entire ghostly conversation), is in most respects, it seems to me, superior. Not so extreme in its characterization, it still obtains the appropriate atmosphere and is a fine, musicianly song. *The Time of Parting* is less involved, less dramatic in treatment, but no less effective.

*Portraits* (1919), a cycle of five poems by Walter de La Mare, is perhaps David Stanley Smith's (1877-) most notable contribution to our song literature. Of these *Portraits, Rachel,* and *The Scarecrow* are the most successful. The former is a thoughtful, subjective song with a well-defined atmosphere. *The Scarecrow* is a clever bit of characterization of entirely different type. The earlier *Love's Music* (Philip Bourne Marston), 1907, has fine dramatic sweep and fervor.

Probably no song-writer among us has enjoyed greater popular success than has Richard Hageman (1882-), with his picturesque songs *At the Well* (1919), *May Night* (1917) and *Do not Go, My Love* (1917), all to Tagore texts. Also *Happi-*

*ness* (Jean Ingelow), 1920, is a fine buoyant song with a remarkably sonorous piano score, as is *Me Company Along* (James Stephens), 1925. Hageman has the happy knack of writing brilliantly, but with no lack of sincerity, albeit, as must be admitted, objectively. The truly subjective song is probably beyond his ken. *Thy Heart is Like a Tomb* (Jacques Boria), 1921, refined and beautiful as it is, is yet perceptibly lacking in human warmth.

Charles Fonteyn Manney (1872-) discloses in his songs an attractive lyricism well exemplified in the cycle of six songs, *A Shropshire Lad*, Op. 22 (A. E. Housman), 1911. His feeling for refined tone color is evidenced in our quotation from the fifth song, *With rue my heart is laden*. His later song *Then Finish the Last Song* (Tagore), 1922, is more dramatically conceived than most of his work.

John Powell (1882-) has published few songs, but *To a Butterfly* and *Phantoms* (1921) are admirable settings of John B. Tabb's fanciful lines. The piano score is rich and elaborate, yet not heavy, expressed indeed with a delightfully light touch.

Of the same type, but showing great advance in technical resource, is *Dawn of Spring*, Op. 25, No. 1 (Karl Burger), 1927. That Mr. Powell can write in more serious vein is well shown in *Frage*, Op. 18, No. 2 (Lenau), 1924. That he is also in constant danger of overcrowding his canvas, of making the vocal line subordinate to mere pianistic display, is evident in all his songs; but nowhere more strikingly shown than in *No*, Op. 25, No. 2 (Karl Burger), 1927, where in the very midst of a song as simple in its content as Schubert's *Heidenröslein* we find a full-chord cadenza which might have come out of a Liszt piano concerto.

In *The Flight of the Moon* (Oscar Wilde), 1914, Carl Deis (1883-) has written a worthy companion piece to Charles T.

A Shropshire Lad — Manney

Griffes' setting of the same text. It is interestingly and poetically conceived throughout. *Two Plaints* for Voice and Piano (1920), *The Waning* (Longfellow) and *A Lover's Lament* (William Martin Johnson) are attractive interpretations of two very diverse moods.

With the attractive song *Palazzo Pagani* (Wilfred Scawen Blunt), 1921, Edward Ballantine (1886-) took his place among the worth-while younger American song-writers. It showed him to be possessed of a rich harmonic sense, excellent craftsmanship, imagination, true musicianship. His first song, it is still perhaps his best.

In 1922 appeared *Lyrics from the Greek*, seven songs in all, the texts translated from the original Greek by Lilla Cabot Perry. These songs skilfully portray various different moods. The opening section of *My Star* is admirable in the simplicity of its treatment, its melodic breadth, and the very real depth of feeling at the words "Ah! would that I might be."

Also in 1922 appeared *The Oak Tree*, another interesting

setting from the same source; in 1926, *Night at the Mission* (J. L. McLane, Jr.).

George Harris delights in elaborate accompanimental patterns which he often uses with excellent effect. In *The Ship Starting* (Walt Whitman), 1925, the "spreading sails," the

My Star — Ballantine

"emulous waves," are skilfully portrayed in this manner.　Simi-larly in *Life is Sweet, Brother* (George Borrow), also 1925, they serve to give pictorial value to the "wind on the heath."　In his later songs, as *Fleet Street* (Shane Leslie), *The Wine-cup* (Richard Aldington) and *Four Tuscan Rispetti*, all 1927, he seems to employ these patterns for sheer pleasure in them as such. Often, as in *Fleet Street*, there is an appropriateness in the mood expressed but the songs are decidedly instrumental rather than vocal, with little attempt at interpretative effect.　*Love's Lily*, perhaps the most successful of the *Rispetti*, is a charming study in purity and delicacy of line.　That it expresses the mood of the poem any further than in this very fragility of style is much to be doubted.　As a song, therefore, its success is open to question; as absolute music it is a delight.

# CHAPTER X

## 1900-1930 (Continued)

*Arthur Bird, Timothy Mather Spelman, Templeton Strong,
Louis Campbell-Tipton, Blair Fairchild*

JUST as we have welcomed Bloch and Loeffler and Boyle into
our own musical fellowship, so in turn we have helped contribute to the musical culture of other lands.   Templeton Strong since
1892 at Vevey and Geneva, Blair Fairchild since 1903 at Paris,
Arthur Bird from 1886 up to his death (1924) at Berlin, Louis
Campbell-Tipton from 1905 until his death in 1921 at Paris,
Timothy Mather Spelman established in Italy—these are some
of our distinguished sons and brothers who in Europe are considered American, in America almost as Europeans.   With their
works published and performed in Europe, with their musical
ties firmly established there, it is not strange that their names
have but a faintly familiar and distant sound in our ears.

Perhaps the best work of Arthur Bird (1856-1924) is found
in the *Five Songs*, Op. 36 (1896).   Of these songs, the fourth,
*When Cupid is Blind,* is likely the most satisfactory, showing
hints of an unwonted effort to get a little below the surface, bits
of imitative counterpoint, a rather broadly conceived obbligato
melody in the piano-part, glints here and there of unaccustomed
richness in the harmonic scheme.   But even here it fails to penetrate very deeply, it never quite attains to being a truly distinctive or notable song.

So that in place of the meticulous care with which Templeton
Strong or Blair Fairchild works out his problems—the insistence on just the right bit of harmonic color here, the right tonal

nuance there, the delicate adjustment of the one to the other—
in place of this persistent thoughtfulness, developing at times
into a deeply subjective mood, we find in the writing of Arthur
Bird the utmost objectivity.    Nor is it entirely without a certain
attractiveness in its care-free, fluent motion.    At times it is even
brilliant, but it is seldom thoughtful, never in the slightest degree introspective.

It is indeed a far cry from Arthur Bird to Timothy Mather
Spelman (1891-), from the *naïveté* of mid-Victorianism to the
almost belligerent independence of all tradition, so characteristic
of this present close of the first quarter of the twentieth century.

No dissonance is too biting for Spelman, no harmonization too acrid, and yet underlying it all is that feeling for logical
sequence, that ability to follow steadily and unwaveringly one's
chosen path through whatever labyrinth, that is always characteristic of the sincere and conscientious creative worker.    His
songs all give evidence of this fact.    Each is strongly individual,
the mood expression and technical processes constantly changing.    In *The Surf* and *Symbols of Winter* (1924)—all of Spelman's songs are to texts by his wife, Leolyn Louise Everett—we
find the sardonic humor of the former and the dreary, desolate
cold of winter in the latter, admirably suggested.    The dark,
portentous mood of *The Sea Witch* contrasts with the subtle and
filmy character of the *Serenade*, as does the vivid human passion
of *The Curse* with the impersonal, aery *Satyr's Song* (all of
1925).    This last is very attractive in its mood of poetic unreality, so deftly expressed in its unusually effective piano score.
In fact it seems the most unequivocally successful of all Spelman's songs.

Of Templeton Strong, the earliest songs that I know are
*Drei Gesänge*, Op. 32 (1887), *Spinnerlied, Geisternähe* and
*Friedel*—excellent songs, in the then all-prevalent German style.
*Geisternähe* is written with laudable restraint and appropriate

atmosphere, while *Friedel* is attractively spontaneous and buoyant, albeit the diction is at times wrenched out of its proper line to fit the musical idea. In 1892 were published *Three Songs*, Op. 38, this time to Elizabethan texts, *Shall a smile or grateful glance* (William Corkine), *Come, ah come, my life's delight* (Thomas Campion) and *Philon* (William Byrd), again excellent songs of their type, the last two being notable for the charmingly original and effective interludes between the verses. The *Songs of an American Peddler* (1922) show all of Strong's technical skill, the never-failing effectiveness of his writing, and were it not for the bitter cynicism of their texts, original with the composer, would all be notable songs. As it is, *The Brook*,

Songs of an American Peddler—Templeton Strong

Brook, Leaf - - - y dell or dark-est nook,

happily free from this baleful influence, is a captivating piece of work whose piano score illustrates to perfection Strong's frequent delicacy of line and purity of style. Unfortunately, the latest song to come from his pen, *An Indian Chief's Reply* (1926), continues the strain of bitterness we have referred to, and thus is its own undoing.

As in his writing for piano Campbell-Tipton (1877-1921), never surpassed his early *Sonata Heroic,* so in his songs the *Four Sea Lyrics* (1907) remain among his best. To these texts by Arthur Symons he has given very sympathetic and attractive settings. *After Sunset* and *Darkness* are both musicianly songs and skilfully welded together by means of a common phrase introduced into both songs—an effect also carried out in the remaining two songs, *The Crying of Water* and *Requies*, of the same high order. *The Opium-Smoker* and *A Memory*, also of 1907, and also to texts by Arthur Symons, are again admirable. But strangely enough we now enter upon a period of unexpected sterility so far as his songs are concerned. There are plenty of them, to be sure, but they say little and that little for the most part in a distinctly commonplace way: *The Shadows* (1907), *A Spirit Flower* (1908), much sung but nevertheless a mediocre song; *Two Short Love Lyrics*: *Homeward* and *Love's Logic* (1910); *Hymn to the Night* (1910), *All the Words that I Gather* (1911). It is only with the *Two Jester Songs*, Op. 31 (1912), that our composer begins to hark back to his former more distinctive manner. With the *Rhapsodie*, Op. 32, No. 1 (1913) and *Invocation*, Op. 32, No. 2 (1915), he seems once more to have found himself, and these two songs are poetically conceived, dramatic, expressive, musicianly. His last published work, the song *Day's End*, issued the year of his death, 1921, is in his favorite free, recitative style, and there are moments of great expressiveness and beauty.

It is interesting to see how the external life of Louis Campbell-Tipton in many respects has paralleled that of Blair Fairchild (1877-). Born at very nearly the same time, they both took up their permanent abode in Paris in the early nineteen hundreds, where Campbell-Tipton died in 1921 at the age of thirty-four. Happily the parallel ceases here, for Fairchild is still busily writing, with, we hope, many years of composition ahead of him.

But while we have been able to trace this comparatively close parallel in their outward life, no such similarity exists in their inner musical experience. We shall see how constant has been the fluidity of Fairchild's self-expression, how he has taken to himself and made part of himself the varying currents of contemporary musical art. Not so with Campbell-Tipton. His latest work is as his earliest work and conforms to the same general type, with the same excellence and the same defects. While Fairchild shows decided French influence, Campbell-Tipton maintains the German idiom throughout.

In taking up the songs of Blair Fairchild we first note the collection of twenty-six *Canti Popolari Italiani*, issued in five different sets, and running through a number of years as follows: Op. 5 (1901), Op. 14 (1907), Op. 23 (1911), Op. 30 (1912), in which the composer has caught the particular nuance of Italian folk-melody; these followed in 1922 by an additional group of six *Stornelli Toscani*. In 1904 appeared an interesting collection of twelve Persian folk-songs, personally collected by Fairchild. A greater contrast could scarcely be conceived than that between the Italianate melody of the *Canti* and *Stornelli* and these weird melodies of the East.

In *The Baghdad Lover*, a cycle of nine songs, Op. 25 (1911), Fairchild gives free rein to his fondness for whole-tone effects. In *So Much I Love* we find the beginning of the type of song which he afterward developed with striking success —the introspective song with simple melodic line but richly textured piano score. With *What Moon Shall Find Thee* we discover another type in which Fairchild excels—the melody similarly lyric and simple, with the accompaniment now characterized by a definite, but subtle, rhythmic pattern. We shall find excellent use made of this type later on. *Serenade* shows a typical plucked-string accompaniment worthy to be compared with Debussy's *Mandoline*, Brahms' *Ständchen*, and other songs of this type.

For Op. 28 (1911), we return to the *Canti Popolari*, where in the midst of the Italian melody we begin to detect a new note in this particular type, an added richness in the scoring, here and there the elsewhere familiar augmented harmony, once even a fragment of whole-tone melody, but still the fluent Italian line.

Probably a world-wide search for material could scarcely have afforded better practice in writing natural, spontaneous melody than the setting of these songs of Tuscany.

With Op. 30 (1912), we find the final numbers of the *Canti Popolari* in duet form and showing ever-increasing harmonic richness and fullness in the piano score.

With the *Five Greek Sea Prayers*, Op. 35 (1913) we reach the beginning of Fairchild's maturer writing for the solo voice, writing which from now on is convincing, effective, original. These songs are of the type which we come later to identify as the prevailing Fairchild type—characterized by rich, full texture in the piano score, with a harmonization which while never cloying, yet abounds in a full chordal effect with subtle shifting of colors. The melodic line is generally subordinate but never tentative or uncertain; and, of course, at times it asserts its proper independence. Fairchild shows many varieties of technique in the handling of songs, but it is quite evident from its frequent use that this is a favorite type, and well it may be, for he has written many delightful songs in this idiom.

*The Baghdad Lover*, as we have seen, served to indicate the line which he was later to develop so admirably, and the *Greek Sea Prayers* carry it on with ever increasing command of resources. Particularly interesting is *Worship in Spring* with its striking, dissonant climax at the words "or the Sicilian shingle." It is interesting to note that this song's opening phrase "Ocean lies purple in calm" is set to a three-note motif which is to appear and reappear throughout the cycle *Les Quatrains d'Al-Ghazali*, to be considered later.

*Les Amours de Hafiz*, Op. 38 (1914), is a cycle of seven songs of great interest—*Le soir parfumé* being distinguished for its simple and yet rich coloring and the thematic interplay between voice and piano; *Dans la nuit profonde* for its delicacy of line; *Oh regarde-moi* and *Extase* for their clarity and lyricism, the latter as well for a clever opposition of rhythms between voice and piano.

With the *Quatrains d'Al-Ghazali*, Op. 40 (1915), we find his finest endeavors in the field of song. This cycle is typical of the French school and shows an opulence of harmonic effects scarcely surpassed by any French composer, be he Duparc, Chausson, Debussy or whosoever. The recurring motif mentioned a moment ago consists of three ascending seconds, forming 5, 6, 7 of a seventh chord, or 7, 8, 9 of a chord of the ninth, which set against its appropriate seventh or ninth harmony forms a very expressive phrase. It appears for the first time at the words "Viens ô bien aimée" in the first song, *Le Grand Jardin d'Azur*. The second song, *O mon Amour* has as a notable characteristic a certain chromatically vibrating figure in the accompaniment, at once effective and original. The scoring of *Nocturne* is peculiarly rich and full, with a striking fortissimo climax, as superb in its coloring as the not dissimilar closing climax in Duparc's *Phidyle*.

(71)                      Les Quatrains d'Al-Ghazali—Fairchild

fin_____ _____Comme à cette heu - - - re!____

*cresc. molto*

*ff*

In *Aimons-nous et revons* the typical motif dominates the entire song.

Les Quatrains d'Al-Ghazali—Fairchild

(72)

*p bien chanté*

Ai-mons-nous___ et rê-vons___

nous n'au-rons pas tou-jours Ce ciel___ de-vant nos

*Près de l'aimée* and *Heure pâle*, as far as texture and rhythm are concerned are absolutely of the type of the earlier *So Much I Love* and *What Moon Shall Find Thee*, from *The Baghdad Lover*, but naturally much elaborated and enriched. The last pages of *Heure pâle*, beginning "Je rêve d'un amour étrange et sans pareil" are of passing beauty.

Les Quatrains d'Al-Ghazali — Fairchild

Je rê - - ve d'un a - mour é - trange et sans pa-

reil, _____ Fait d'a - do - ra - ti - on très tendre, _____

_____ un peu mys - ti - que, Pres_que sem-blable a des ca-

This entire cycle shows Fairchild's poetic feeling, interesting harmonization, flexibility of declamation, in striking manner.

*Songs from the Chinese* (1922) contains also much that is attractive.   Here we begin to sense the influence of Stravinsky and his school, though *Night* and *Plucking Rushes* are still French in their suavity and charm, the latter, however, glimpsing the newer idiom in certain phrases near the close.   *Deux chants populaires persans* (1922) are scored with the skill and appropriateness we should expect from Fairchild.

The year 1922 saw also the publication of the six *Stornelli Toscani* referred to above, in which the composer has treated his Italian melody with ever increasing sympathy and success.   In 1928 appeared a further continuation of the songs from the Chinese with *The Message*, text from Mei Chang, and a song to English text, *Drifting* (Caroline Duer), both showing in marked degree the refined expression, the free play of color, the harmonic flexibility, so characteristic of Fairchild's later style.

In the two finely differentiated songs, *Coeur Embrasé* and *Nuit d' Été* (both Lahor) 1930, we find once more all these qualities in evidence, and the fiery passion of the first is splendidly delineated (it is perhaps the most dramatically conceived of all Fairchild's songs).   The second, while no less appealing, is quieter and less intense.

Of this same period are the following composers, with again a few recent representative songs:

LOUIS ADOLPHE COERNE, 1870-1922
   *I Rise from Dreams of Thee* (Shelley), 1921

PERCY LEE ATHERTON, 1871

FREDERICK S. CONVERSE, 1871
   *My April Lady* (Van Dyke), 1909

BERTRAM SHAPLEIGH, 1871

RUBIN GOLDMARK, 1872
   *Four Songs*, Op. 5 (1900)

G. A. GRANT-SCHAEFER, 1872
  French-Canadian Songs, 1921

D. G. MASON, 1873
  Cycle—*Russians* (Witter Binner), 1920

H. CLOUGH-LEIGHTER, 1874
  *My Lover, He Comes on the Skee* (H. H. Boyesen), 1901

GILBERT SPROSS, 1874

HALLET GILBERTÉ, 1875

OLEY SPEAKS, 1876

MORTIMER WILSON, 1876
  *Four Songs,* Op. 59, 1920

HARRIET WARE, 1877

JOHN PRINDLE SCOTT, 1877

CLAUDE WARFORD, 1877

MABEL W. DANIELS, 1878
  *Glory and Endless Years* (Howells), 1921

STANLEY R. AVERY, 1879

FRANK LA FORGE, 1879
  *Song of the Open* (Jessica Hawley Lowell), 1919

J. H. DENSMORE, 1880

ERIC DE LAMATER, 1880
  *Love-Free* (Sara Teasdale), 1920

HOMER GRUNN, 1880

ALEXANDER RUSSELL, 1880
  *The Fountain Court* (Arthur Symons), 1916

MARSHALL KERNOCHAN, 1880
  *Wanderchild,* 1922

GENA BRANSCOMBE, 1881
  *The Best is Yet to Be* (Browning), 1921

F. MORRIS CLASS, 1881

CHARLES WAKEFIELD CADMAN, 1881

HARVEY B. GAUL, 1881
  *While the West is Paling* (W. E. Henley), 1926

OSCAR E. SCHMINKE, 1881
  *Thou Hast Made Me Endless*⎱ (Tagore), 1924
  *The Light of Love*          ⎰

ARTHUR BERGH, 1882

RALPH COX, 1884
*April-tide* (Clinton Scollard), 1917

JAMES P. DUNN, 1884

LOUIS GRUENBERG, 1884
*A Fantasy* (Bliss Carman), 1922

HAROLD HENRY, 1884

CECIL BURLEIGH, 1885 '

CHARLES HUERTER, 1885

WARREN STOREY SMITH, 1885
*A Caravan from China Comes* (R. Le Gallienne), 1920

REGINALD SWEET, 1885

DEEMS TAYLOR, 1885
*Three Songs*, Op. 13 (James Stephens), 1920

HAROLD V. MILLIGAN, 1886
*Five Lyrics* from Sara Teasdale, 1917

EDWARD S. BARNES, 1887

WALTER GOLDE, 1887
*Sudden Light* (Rossetti), 1921
*April Light* (Ruth Oliver), 1924
*To an Invalid* (Mary MacDougall), 1924

W. FRANKE HARLING, 1887

WALTER MORSE RUMMEL, 1887

LILY STRICKLAND, 1887

LUCILE CREWS, 1888
*Nocturne* (Clinton Scollard), 1918
*Three Oriental Miniatures*, 1926

ALBERT SPALDING, 1888
*Four Songs from The Hesperides* (Herrick), 1924

C. HUGO GRIMM, 1890
*May-dew* (Samuel Lover), 1920

PHILIP JAMES, 1890
*The Victory Riders* (Theodosia Garrison), 1920

WILLIAM REDDICK, 1890
*Two Loves* (Charles Hanson Towne), 1918

DAGMAR DE CORVAL RYBNER, 1890
*Au Piano* (Jean Lahor), 1921
*A Song* (Clinton Scollard), 1925
*Chanson de Grand-Père* (Victor Hugo), 1925

KAROLYN WELLS BASSETT, 1892

ALBERT STOESSEL, 1894

HOWARD BARLOW
*Hush of the World* (Maxwell S. Burt), 1923
*The Garden* (Paul H. Bonner), 1924

EUGENE BONNER

CHARLES S. BURNHAM

PEARL CURRAN

FANNIE C. DILLON

HENRY EICHHEIM
*Seven Songs,* 1910

CHARLES FERRY
*June* (Arthur Guiterman), 1919

FAY FOSTER

J. BERTRAM FOX
*A Ballad* (Maurice Baring), 1921
*Eventide* (Charlotte Bronte), 1921
*Two Songs from Chinese*

HENRY S. GERSTLÉ
*Spring Sadness* (Helen Valentine), 1922

ELLIOT GRIFFIS
*A Caravan from China Comes* (R. Le Gallienne), 1920

RICHARD HAMMOND
*Elizabethan Love Songs,* Op. 13, 1921

GORDON HATFIELD
*Cycle of Wistful Songs* (after Goethe), 1921

FRANCIS HENDRICKS

CONSTANCE MILLS HERRESHOFF
  Cycle—*Miniature Recital Songs*, 1921

KATHERINE HEYMAN

MABEL WOOD HILL

ROSALIE HOUSMAN
  *A Cry of the Orient*, 1922

HORACE JOHNSON
  *Thy Dark Hair* (James Mahoney), 1920
  *Fragments*, 1924
  *A Fair Lady* (Helen Redington), 1925

EASTWOOD LANE

A. A. MACK
  *April* (William Matson), 1904
  *The Enchantress* (Bliss Carman), 1904

MANA-ZUCCA

CHARLES H. MARSH
  *Three Hills* (Everard Owen), 1922

MARY CARR MOORE

ARTHUR CLEAVELAND MORSE
  *Love Sings a Song* (F. H. Martens), 1922

ALEXANDER MACFADYEN
  *Slender Your Hands* (Joyce Kilmer), 1925
  *The Reveille* (Minna Irving), 1925

CARL MCKINLEY
  *Reverie* (Franz Lee Rickaby), 1927
  *The Nightingale Has a Lyre of Gold* (W. E. Henley), 1927

HOWARD D. MCKINNEY

H. O. OSGOOD

SENECA PIERCE

CHARLES REPPER
  *Dusk* (Seumas O'Sullivan), 1919
  *In the Garden of the World* (G. Baronti), 1919
  *Song Is So Old* (Hermann Hagedorn), 1919

GERTRUDE ROSS
  *Early Spanish-American Folk Songs*, 1922

EDWARD ROYCE
  *Evening Star* (Poe), 1922

FRANK ST. LEGER
*The Unknowing* (Theodosia Garrison), 1919
*Three Songs from the Arabian* (Toussaint), 1920

HOMER SAMUELS
*Pierrot* (Sara Teasdale), 1922

META SCHUMANN

RHEA SILBERTA
*Yohrzeit* (Silberstein), 1919
*Yom Kippur* (Silberstein), 1921

DONALD TWEEDY
*The Little Angels of Heaven* (Ford Madox Hueffer), 1923

RUTH WRIGHT VANDERLIP
*A Vagabond Song* (Bliss Carman), 1926

Similarly, coming to us from other lands:

WILLIAM H. BERWALD, 1864

LOUIS KOEMMENICH, 1866

SIGISMOND STOJOWSKI, 1870
*Euphonies,* Six Songs, Op. 33

BRYCESON TREHARNE, 1879

KURT SCHINDLER, 1882

WILLIAM LESTER, 1889
Cycle—*Along the Hwang-Ho* (Frederick H. Martens), 1921

WERNER JOSTEN
*Through the Silver Moon,* 1921
*The Windflowers,* 1922

and many others.

# CHAPTER XI

## 1900-1930 (CONTINUED)

### *Wintter Watts, John Alden Carpenter*

AND now, having taken this birds-eye view of the whole broad field of American song and in order that we may penetrate still more deeply into its spirit, not at all as Francis Hopkinson conceived it, nor as Parker, or Pease, or Buck, or Bartlett, but as it is being written in our very midst today, let us take for the purposes of this somewhat more intimate study, a small, compact group of representative writers, a survey of whose works may help to bring before us something of a composite picture of the various aspects of American song of today, or, perhaps, to speak more exactly, of American song of the past decade.

I have chosen Alice Barnett (1888-), John Alden Carpenter (1876-), Bainbridge Crist (1883-), Charles T. Griffes (1884-1920), A. Walter Kramer (1890-) and Wintter Watts (1884-), as perhaps best representing, both as regards the quality and quantity of their work, this cross section of contemporary American song.

And I have further chosen to discuss the songs of Wintter Watts first, because more than any other in this group he seems to me to be thoroughly American in his work. It may well prove difficult to maintain this thesis to the satisfaction of others, for of course it is a very intangible thing—this expression of one's nationality in his art. And again perhaps I shall find it even more difficult to defend my second proposition—namely, that of this group, John Alden Carpenter is the least American!

And this in the face of some one's declaration not long since that there is something essentially American about all his work. Now this does not mean that the Americanism of the one, or the non-Americanism of the other, betokens greater or less ability. That is entirely beside the question and does not enter into the contention at all. But Wintter Watts from the very beginning has seemed to embody in his songs many of our outstanding American characteristics. Even his earliest songs, Op. 2, 3 and 4, are American to the core in the abounding enthusiasm which so evidently went into their construction. More often than not this enthusiasm was entirely misdirected, even into the most extravagant modes of expression. Imagine, for instance, Arthur Symons' pathetic *Dreams* set to music of the most flamboyant type! It is youth, it is enthusiasm, and it is American! It took years of time and much experience to overcome this element of the over-obvious in his work; and one cannot say that it is even now entirely eliminated. But for the most part it has been transformed into a certain richness of texture which is very engaging. Subtle it may not be, but effective—and American!

Watts' writing, from its beginning even up to the present, has never been distinguished for its originality; one is always coming upon something that has a familiar flavor, as in *The Golden Rose*, one of his loveliest songs, where we find the rhythm and general mood of a part of Wagner's Scene of the Flower Maidens reproduced almost literatim. But there are so many excellences in his songs that one would be a captious critic indeed who would dwell at length upon their minor defects.

And the fine thing about his writing is that it has been broadening and developing with the years. His last songs are his best songs. His craftmanship has become increasingly sure, so that we may feel entire confidence that what he writes will be well written, as far as the technique of writing is concerned. His Americanism shows itself among other things in a direct, aboveboard mode of expression. He still has a fondness for some particular effects of a distinctly objective type, indicating a certain ingenuousness in his artistic make-up, which stands in no awe of those who would charge him with doing the straightforward, everyday thing, of being less sophisticated then he might be. American again!

If we wish to study his songs somewhat in detail, we can perhaps best begin with *Like Music on the Waters* (Byron), published in 1908. This song is neither strikingly original nor modern in feeling, but so close knit is its texture, so smooth its contrapuntal weave, that in a sober, serious sort of way it is one of his most effective songs. The year 1919 was his banner year as far as publication is concerned, eight songs beside the cycle *Vignettes of Italy* having been issued in this year alone, and what is most important in the matter, all of them distinctive songs. *The Poet Sings* is to a text by Richard Le Gallienne, while two others and the above-mentioned cycle (nine songs in all) are settings of poems by Sara Teasdale. It is really remarkable to what extent her poems have been made use of in recent American song. Indeed, it is quite certain that if our younger American song-writers were to enter upon a plebiscite as to who should be crowned Poet Laureate in the kingdon of song, there would be no doubt as to the outcome; their votes ha already been cast in their songs. *The Poet Sings, Love Me* and *Pierrot* (these also to Sara Teasdale texts) are all effective bits of lyricism, each with its own distinctive appeal. In *Vignettes of Italy* we come to one of Watts' most ambitious productions and thoroughly typical of his art. It is quite American in the elemental simplicity of its harmonic background (there is no impressionistic vagueness here), and the effects are gained by the most objective means. For this reason it is easy to see why the less subjective parts of the text are best realized; for instance, one of the most interesting things in the entire cycle is the bell clangor in *Ponte Vecchio, Florence,* and this is exceedingly artistic in its presentment.   There is nothing commonplace about it—it may well be compared with Debussy's *Les Cloches,* nor fear the comparison.

Vignettes of Italy — Watts

The forthrightness of his style does not lend itself easily to the expression of the more subtle moods and feelings, and hence *Capri* is disappointing. However, there are some attractive nuances in *Addio* and *Stresa* which produce a certain sympathetic plasticity of mood, notably at the words "When unexpected beauty burns like sudden sunlight" in the first

Vignettes of Italy.—Watts

on _____ the sea, _____

and "The lake is a dreamy bride" in the last.

Vignettes of Italy—Watts

The lake _____ is a

dream - y bride _____

The *Piu mosso* here also is well worked out.   Throughout the
cycle we find Watts' favorite devices, the bold ⁶⁄₄ climax, the
broad Brahms-like turn in the melody, and at "dewy flower"
in *Naples* and "stars what I" in *Night Song at Amalfi*, one of
his pet uses of the subdominant harmony,

(77)                                        Vignettes of Italy—Watts

I ask'd the heav'n___      of  stars What I      should give,

for Watts is one of those composers not afraid to make use of the
frank, open character of this chord.   He uses it repeatedly in
this and kindred ways.   To be sure, one comes to look for it and
it is probably overdone, but in many instances he derives great
beauty from its use.

Again, in the *Five Songs* published this same year we find
much of interest.   *Utopia* (Frances Turner Palgrave) is once
most typical of Watts in his most accustomed mood.   It is exceedingly solid in its harmonic structure, non-futuristic to a
degree, and while seemingly made up of familiar material, is suf-
fused with such charm of color that it seems far from commonplace.   Indeed, this seems to be one of Watts' fundamentally
American characteristics—to take a perfectly familiar harmonic
formula and so color it that while possessing all the personal
interest of the known, the familiar, it is yet illumined by some
rarer light than that of common every day; a very happy com-

bination, for when all is said and done we Americans are most of us not particularly adventurous in our art tastes; we do not want to go too far afield.  In *Golden Rose* (Grace Hazard Conkling) we find the harmonization a bit more sophisticated and of great beauty; it is only unfortunate, as we said above, that its parallel sixths should be so reminiscent of Wagner's Flower Maidens.  Of still more piquant harmonic and rhythmic interest is *The Little Shepherd's Song* (13th century, Wm. Alexander Percy), 1922, while in *A Little Page's Song* (same authorship), 1920, a song of equal attractiveness but of entirely different technique, he reverts to his usual style.  It is an exceedingly winsome song and the music mirrors to a nicety the naïveté of the text. *Tryste Noël* (Louise Imogen Guiney), 1921, shows once more the skill with which Watts is able to transfigure the simplest material.  Here again the quaintness of the text has found full and sympathetic realization in the music.  Quite at the opposite pole from these songs is *Joy* (1922), to the well-known verses of Sara Teasdale.  Its exuberance is a fit contrast to the wistful pathos of the Noël.  Between the two comes *Wings of Night*

(Sara Teasdale), 1921, one of the most poetic of all Watts' songs, and containing at the words "My heart, like the bird in the tree," one of those meaty harmonic progressions that we find so often in the songs of Brahms. This might well have been written by that master himself. *With the Tide* (Edward J. O'Brien), 1922, is, also, thoroughly characteristic; in fact, its first phrase might be said actually to epitomize Watts' style. Here is a superb, sweeping phrase for the voice, in bold outline, and with the characteristic broad turn and the equally characteristic leaning toward the subdominant in its underlying harmony, exceedingly effective and exceedingly unoriginal; and yet this underlying harmony is so skilfully handled and its outlines so softened that it is tranformed from what could so

float— be - yond— the wa - ters of— the

world. The

easily have become commonplace into something really admirable. Throughout the song the surge of the sea is excellently suggested, and the harmonic color becomes richer and richer, closing with one of Watts' most brilliant cadences. *The Nightingale and the Rose* (William Ernest Henley), 1922, is a striking song, developed *à la* Rimsky-Korsakoff with excellent success. It is decidedly no mere imitation. The long and elaborate prelude serves admirably to establish the mood of the song and to show once again Watts' unusual skill in adapting well-worn formulæ to modern uses. Note the sequence at the words "While she triumphs waxing frail, fading even while she glows" with its combination of modern harmony and rhythmic freedom with good old-fashioned counterpoint:

The Nightingale and the Rose —Watts

While she tri - umphs, wax - ing frail,____ Fad-ing

e - -ven while____ she glows:

A song of very different type is *Intreat Me Not to Leave Thee* (text from the book of Ruth). Here we find the note of pathos, not often struck in Watts' songs. The tenderness of "or to return from following after thee" is very genuine;

Intreat me not to leave thee —Watts

and the strange, half-barbaric march immediately following, set against the broadest kind of sustained phrase in the voice-part, is effective and original. The declamation is notable for its breadth and dignity, giving a distinctly heroic touch to the song as a whole. Aside from these two songs of larger calibre, Watts' later songs have all been of a more intimate, subjective type than his earlier works; of compact structure for the most part, and with skilfully written and easy-flowing counterpoint, imitative and otherwise, as in *Only a Cry* (Sara Teasdale) and *Only and Forever* (William Ernest Henley), both 1923, with the deliberate longbreathed phrases so characteristic of his later songs. As we note the increasingly rich scoring in all these songs, we can but regret the lack of originality and freedom in the construction of his melodies. If his melodic invention were equal to his skill in harmonization and general all-round craftsmanship, his songs would rank very high indeed. Perhaps as free from this fault as any of these later songs is the tender, meditative *Transformation* (Jessie B. Rittenhouse), 1922, but even here a most conventional cadence in the voice-part but seems to emphasize this criticism. *Bring Her Again to Me* (Henley), 1923, is notable for a very interestingly developed and novel pictorial touch at the words "Over the western sea," where various superimposed octaves in the bass, sustained by means of the pedal and so blending the one into another, give a unique feeling of watery depth;

Bring Her Again to Me — Watts

and *Wild Tears* (Louise Imogen Guiney), 1923, is distinguished
for a weird kind of cadenza, recurring in the voice-part with
very telling effect; the closing cadence is deeply felt and of great
poignancy.

Wild Tears—Watts

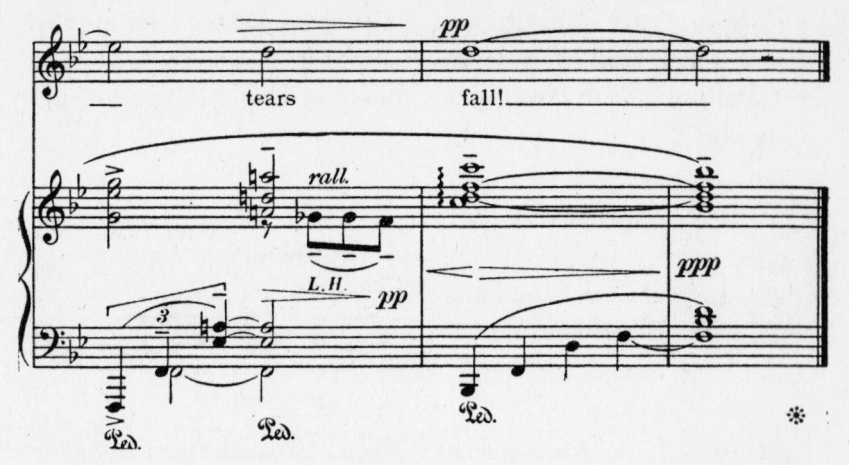

tears    fall!

*Let it be Forgotten* (Sara Teasdale), 1923, although having passages of great beauty, is on the whole less original in its construction, while *A White Rose* (John Boyle O'Reilly), 1923, shows an entirely different type of technique, its score consisting for the most part of delicate arabesque figures admirably adapted to the piano, and enwreathing the melody as a rose is embowered in its own leafage.    It is one of Watts' most delightfully lyric songs, and shows also the various earmarks of his particular style.

Of *Three Songs for Low Voice* (1924), two, *Song is so Old* (Herman Hagedorn) and *Dark Hills* (Edwin Arlington Robinson) are conspicuously successful examples of his growing tendency toward the more intimate, atmospheric type of song; and while suffering no diminution in the richness of their harmonic background, show a distinct gain in melodic freedom and originality of treatment.    The third member of this group, *Miniver Cheevy* (also Edwin Arlington Robinson), is as cleverly whimsical as its text!

The more I have studied Watts' individuality as expressed in his songs, the more I am impressed with the thought of his Americanism. There is first of all the forthrightness, the open and aboveboard genuineness, the directness of approach, the willingness to make use of anything which comes to hand, the personal independence which leads him to employ certain effects whether they happen to be in the mode or not—all this, I feel sure, is easily recognizable as belonging to our national temperament. On the other hand, the absence of any tendency toward mysticism, reluctance to dwell very much on the emotional element, avoidance of the sentimental or the slightest hint of the lachrymose—that is Wintter Watts and that, I am confident, is American.

Surely, 1912 was a memorable year in American Song, for during this year appeared John Alden Carpenter's first published songs, namely, *Eight Songs for a Medium Voice* and the *Four Poems* by Paul Verlaine, with yet another setting of a Verlaine text, *Where the Misty Shadows Glide*. It is much to be doubted if any other year has brought forth quite so rich a fruitage. They are to be envied who first saw these songs fresh from the press, for there is no question that with them was ushered in a new era in American song literature. Here spoke a new voice, permeated with French influence, to be sure, but yet thoroughly individual and with something definite to say, together with great skill in the saying of it. Think of these thirteen songs with not a single weak one among them! It is true that Carpenter published two other songs this same year, but they are evidently much earlier, for while they are not without a certain excellence—*May, the Maiden* (Sidney Lanier) has much to commend it—still they seem to lack every evidence of that striking personality so apparent in all the other songs. But among these thirteen under review there is not one unworthy song, and they exhibit great versatility in technique and mood expression. In 1913 these were followed by *Four Songs for a Medium Voice*, in 1914, by *Gitanjali* (Tagore), in 1915, two detached songs, in 1916, *Water Colors* (from the Chinese), then various scattered songs; and in 1921, *Two Night Songs* (Siegfried Sassoon), in 1927, *Four Negro Songs*, in 1930, a Song for Medium Voice, *Young Man, Chieftain.*   So that in the five years, from 1912 to 1916 inclusive, there appeared altogether thirty-one songs—a remarkable record when we consider their great value and varied content.   More than any other American song-composer he seems to have sprung forth fully equipped, to have been sure of himself at the very outset.   So that in justice to Carpenter one must begin his study with the first published songs. If we start with his *Eight Songs*, we find in the first one—*The Green River* (Lord Alfred Douglas)—a fine instance of his sure skill in all that goes to make up song technique: a keen harmonic sense, exceedingly plastic and capable of being molded with the utmost freedom; charming bits of melody, fashioned with the greatest refinement of line and content; invariable correspondence of text with its embodying music—and whatever else you will, for it is all there!   What poetry lies in the suggestion of the "winding path" by means of these sinuous chromatic harmonies, the glints of melody and the harp-like figures suggestive of the unheard music, the expressive recitative at the words "And all the unravished silence belong to some sweet singer—lost or unrevealed," passing out in harmonies fittingly vague and indeterminate;

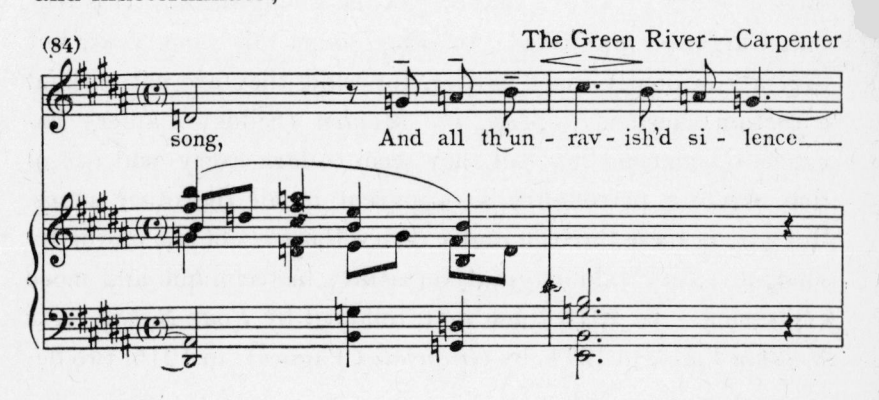

(84)                                    The Green River—Carpenter

song,          And all th'un - rav - ish'd si - lence

be-long To some sweet sing-er

lost, or un-re - vealed.

the longing of "Oh, may I awake from this uneasy night," where the color of the harmonic background, the very intervals of the vocal phrase, the figuration of the accompaniment, all tend to emphasize just the right mood; and all this bringing us to the climacteric suggestion of the "music manifold," with its long melodic line and broad harmonization. The close is exquisite with its bit of whole-tone color leading into "or else delight, that is as wide-eyed as a marigold." With this closing phrase, however, I have never been able to reconcile the cloying harmonies in the accompaniment. The melodic line is perfect, but the harmonization has always seemed to me to be appropriate to the richest orchid—anything rather than a wide-eyed marigold! But that is a negligible defect, in the midst of so much that is supremely good.

I have gone into this song with a fair amount of detail, for it is so entirely characteristic of Carpenter's method of procedure throughout all his songs.　He may not think of himself as belonging to the psychological or "panoramic" school of songwriters—but be that as it may, we have no composer more expert

(85) Più animato　　　　　　　　　The Green River——Carpenter

Oh,＿＿ may I a - wake＿＿ from this un-
ea - sy night.＿＿
To find some voice of mu - - - sic

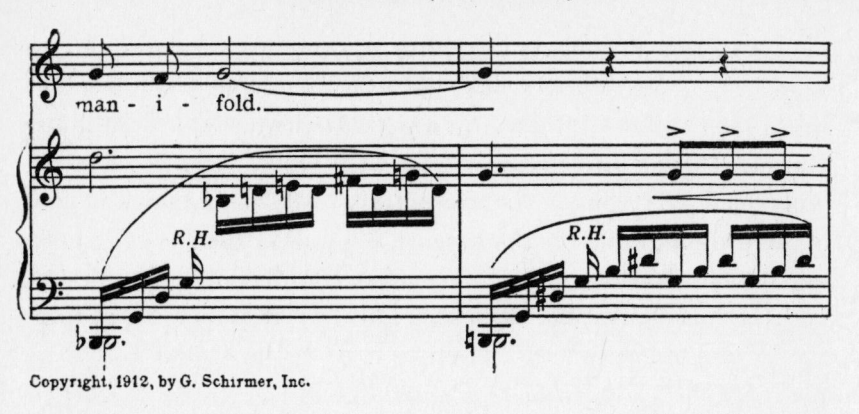

at fitting the tone to the word than he; and herein lies much of his strength as a composer of songs.

The Green River—Carpenter

(86)

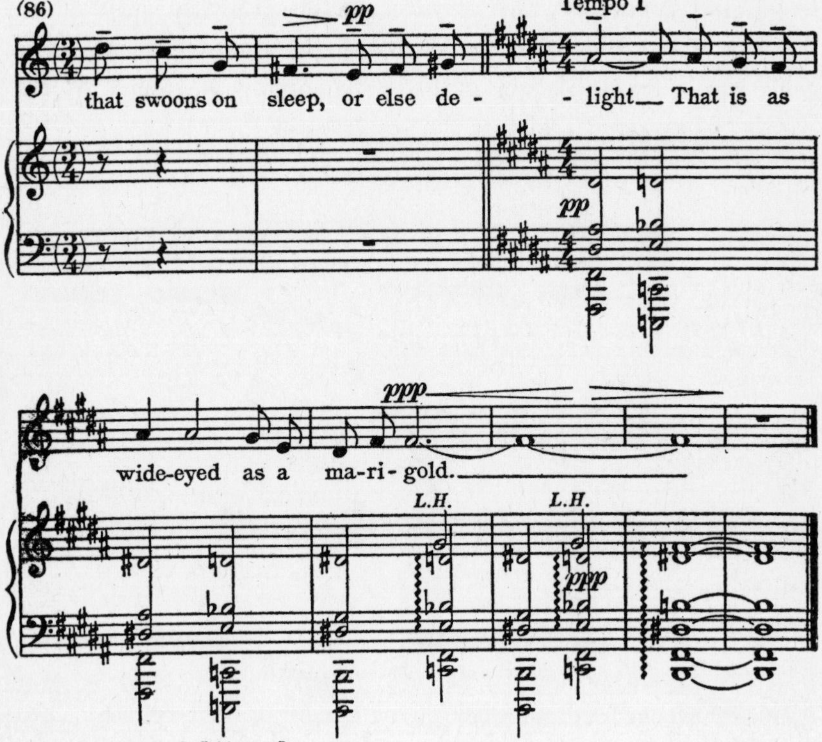

Although in general anything in song that borders on the humorous is my own personal pet aversion, I must admit a certain liking for *Don't Ceäre*, in which Carpenter has set William Barnes' Dorsetshire dialect verses with really remarkable skill. The voice-part runs on in characteristically monotonous monologue fashion, while the piano score abounds in the most fascinating double rhythms and the merriest counterpoint imaginable, and the harmonization, although appropriately simple, is anything but commonplace. If there must be humorous songs, or those bordering thereon, may they all be graced with the art of *Don't Ceäre*.

*Looking-Glass River* (Robert Louis Stevenson) is rich in carillon effects of great attractiveness, while *Go, Lovely Rose* (Edmund Waller) is one of the most ingratiating songs of the group. I imagine Wintter Watts would almost envy Carpenter's clever manipulation of his subdominant harmony at the words "How sweet and fair she seems to be."

Go, Lovely Rose—Carpenter

The middle section with its weirdly conceived harmonies cut into solid blocks, as it were, might have come from Cyril Scott. The two Blake poems, *Little Fly* and *A Cradle-Song*, receive sympathetic treatment, the former particularly attractive by reason of its filmy, unsubstantial harmonization, the latter for its simplicity and artistic restraint—a model for this much abused type of song.

In the first of his four Verlaine songs, *Chanson d'Automne*, we find another example of that meditative type of song apparently so dear to his heart. Here, as so many times, we find flowering out of the very midst of a quiet, neutral background some broad, expressive melodic phrase in the piano-part, as at the words "Tout suffocant et blême,"

(88)                                                                    Chanson d'Automne—Carpenter

And breath-less pain Is mine, while time Is creep-ing,
*Tout suf - fo - cant et blê - me   quand son - ne l'heu- re,*

vitalizing it much as the introduction of the human figure serves to give life to the painted landscape. *Le ciel* is an exceptionally perfect bit of atmospheric writing, the antiphonal effects and suggestions of bell tones being managed with rare skill, while at the close there emerges from the shadows one of those typical Carpenterese glints of melody, bringing us at once from the world of unrealities into that of human experience. In *Dansons la gigue* we find again Carpenter's dexterity in employing simultaneously two different rhythmical schemes, this time waltz rhythms in both $\frac{2}{4}$ and $\frac{3}{8}$ time. *Il pleure dans mon coeur* is a dull grey montone, effective because of its very monotony. *Where the Misty Shadows Glide*, one of his loveliest Verlaine settings, shows the naturalness with which Carpenter's melodies develop. Could anything be less studied or artificial than the evolution and development of the initial melody in this song?

When the misty shadows glide — Carpenter

(89) Slowly and in pensive mood

When the mist-y shad-ows glide,
Cal - mes dans le de - mi - jour

At the tran-quil end of day,
que les bran-ches hau - tes font,

Then let the soul of
pé - né - trons bien

si - lence come,
no - tre a - mour

And in our love a - bide.
de ce si - len - ce pro - fond.

It is this unconscious logic in his musical thinking that so often gives Carpenter's songs their sense of spontaneity and inevitableness.

Les Silhouettes — Carpenter

In the four songs published in 1913 we find further evidence of this logical development, this inevitability.   Directly in the first song, *Les Silhouettes* (Oscar Wilde), the germ of the whole work, as far as its accompanimental background is concerned, appears at once: a group of three chords, rugged three-note chords, two of the three built up of superimposed fourths, in dotted rhythm, two longer chords separated by the shorter; and this motif, slight as it is, dominates the entire song.   And even though at times it may seem to have entirely disappeared, its rhythm at least is present to the very end.   It is a striking instance of the economy of means to which, when he wishes, Carpenter is able to confine himself; and naturally the song is unified thereby as would scarcely be possible in any other way. *Her Voice* (also Oscar Wilde) is one of Carpenter's most fluent and facile songs, although the voice-part maintains its long, deliberate line.   It may be questioned, perhaps, whether a somewhat more dramatic treatment of the voice in this instance would not have still further heightened the emotional value of the song.   *To One Unknown* (Helen Dudley) contains one of those passages of rich sonority in which Carpenter is so successful.   It occurs at the words "I have kissed the shining feet of Twilight, loverwise, opened the gates of Dawn."   Effective as it is, it cannot be said to be in any way strikingly original either in its means or manner, and in this way differs from the tremendous climax in *Light, My Light,* soon to be considered.   But in its own way it is of exceeding dramatic value and again exemplifies Carpenter's admirable economy of means, the entire passage of six very full measures being built up upon only three major chords, but enriched by a wealth of chromatic octaves, wide-flung arpeggios and the like.   *Fog Wraiths* (Mildred Howells) is an imaginative and suggestive treatment of its text.

When we reach *Gitanjali*, a setting of various Tagore texts, we come to one of Carpenter's most important works. I suspect that no one of all the myriad interpreters of Tagore has more truly caught his spirit. At any rate these songs are distinctive, original, not to be surpassed among the best American songs. The rich texture of *When I bring you coloured toys*, the solemnity of *On the day when death will knock at thy door*, the tenderness of *The sleep that flits on baby's eyes*, the poesy of *I am like a remnant of a cloud of Autumn* with its finely developed climax at "paint it with colors, gild it with gold, float it on the wanton winds and spread it in varied wonders"—

all these serve really as but preliminary to the supreme achievement of the last two songs, *On the Seashore of Endless Worlds,* and *Light, my Light.* In the first of these Carpenter has succeeded in transmuting the fragility and transparent beauty of the child-spirit into tones, as I remember it to have been done only in Pierné's *Children's Crusade.* Could anything be more felicitous than the setting of the passage beginning "while children gather pebbles and scatter them again?"

Gitanjali — Carpenter

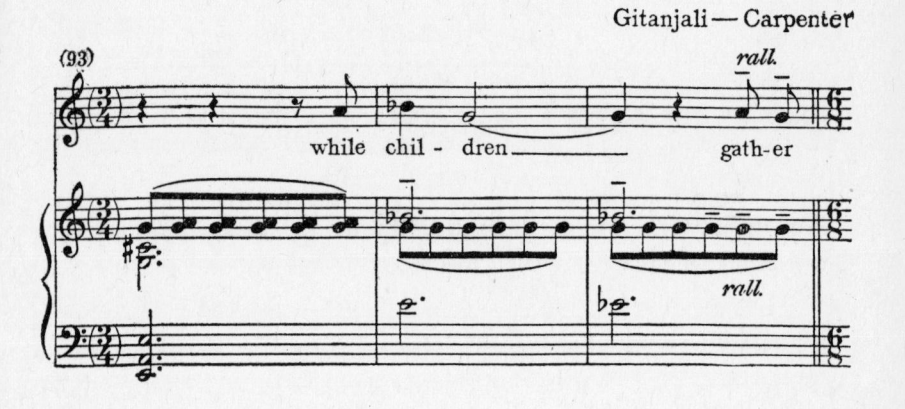

peb - bles____     and scat-ter them a -

gain._____     They seek not for hid - den

treas-ures, ____     they know not   how to   cast     nets.____

Throughout the song the simplicity of the means employed is in remarkable contrast with the effect attained.   In vividly contrasting mood is the brilliant pæan of praise to *Light, my Light.* Here is no slender threadlike melodic line, but great bursts of golden tone like the full-throated voice of the orchestra.   It is no song in the true sense of the word, but a flaming forth of elemental ecstasy. I know of nothing like it. It is written for no mortal voice. Perhaps archangelic voices might cope with its long-drawn trumpet-like phrases, but no earthly voice should attempt these soaring flights! Passing by *The Day is No More* (also Tagore), with its wealth of oriental mysticism, and the imaginative setting of W. B. Yeats' *The Player-Queen*, we come to *Water Colors*, a cycle of Chinese tone-poems, which with *Gitanjali* probably represents Carpenter's work at its very best. Here is the same clever interpretation of the text, the invariable refinement of style—it seems that Carpenter has forgotten (if he ever knew!) how to write a commonplace phrase. Even his title is chosen with rare skill, for "water colors" is just what they are—there is none of the gorgeousness characterizing so many of the songs in *Gitanjali* (*Light, my Light* was painted in oils and with broad brushwork if ever a song were), but here everything is done with the utmost delicacy and with all the tints and half-tints so characteristic of this particular medium. If there be no thrills, there is at least constant charm. *The Odalisque* and *To a Young Gentleman*—could there be anything more graceful than the one, or more whimsically human than the other? Or was there ever a closing cadence more weirdly fascinating than that of *On a Screen* (see Ex. 94)?

Of his more important songs there remain still to be mentioned the two settings of verses by Siegfried Sassoon, *Slumber-Song* and *Serenade*, the *Four Negro Songs* (Langston Hughes) and *Young Man Chieftain* (Mary Austin). *Slumber-Song*, while giving many glimpses of Carpenter's customary ability, seems to lack his usual sense of cohesion and unity; it sounds diffuse, loose-jointed. The *Serenade*, on the other hand, is closely knit, unified throughout. It is full of perverse rhythms, its mood is rather distraught, but it is a powerful song, well put together, with all of Carpenter's facility in craftsmanship. In the *Four Negro Songs:*

(94) Tempo I *p* Water-colors — Carpenter

A tor-toise I see⸺ on a

lo - tus - flow- er⸺ rest - - ing.⸺

poco accel.

a tempo

*Shake your brown feet, honey, The Cryin' Blues, Jazz-Boys* and
*That Soothin' Song,* Carpenter shows that jazz rhythms may be
used with artistic effect and once again gives proof that whatever he turns his hand to gains distinction thereby. Here are
various moods presented, each with its appropriate atmosphere.
Extraordinarily impressive in its rugged strength is the Indian
Prayer, *Young Man Chieftain.* We feel at once the innate man-
liness of this Indian youth, and the music with all its wild uncouthness breathes a serious dignity most appealing. Debussy
could scarcely have bettered the phrase, "Lord of the small rain."
(Nature again!) It is a powerful song, original, effective.

To sum up, I find in Carpenter, to a greater extent than
in the case of any other American song-writer, the meditative

spirit, the love of expressing the genius of nature, the out-of-doors, in its quieter aspects and in its influence upon human experience. We need but recall *Where the Misty Shadows Glide, Chanson d' Automne, Le Ciel, Il pleure dans mon coeur, The Green River, Looking-Glass River, The Cock shall Crow, Les Silhouettes, Fog Wraiths, On the Seashore of Endless Worlds, Light, my Light, The Day is No More, Water Colors* and *Slumber-Song.* Surely no other among our composers has been so drawn in this direction. This sympathetic reaction to the moods of nature has been, perhaps, my chief point in feeling a certain non-Americanism in Carpenter's work. Any one who knows this inborn love of the out-of-doors in its more subjective moods, so characteristic of many peoples of the earth, and so uncharacteristic of our own, to whom the out-of-doors means pure objectivity—an auto ride or a baseball game—will understand what I mean. We may acquire this sincere love of nature and it is to be hoped that most of us do, but it is a matter not lightly to be taken for granted. That Carpenter has felt this so keenly, serves at once to set him aside from most of his colleagues. To my mind, songs of this type are the most beautiful and companionable of all types, but not to every composer is it given to write them worthily. To Brahms it was given in perhaps the fullest measure ever granted, and we may well congratulate ourselves that in Carpenter we find one so worthily following where he led.

Then, too, the aristocratic elegance of his style, oversophisticated it may be at times (but seldom)—that is non-American; as is his perfection of finish and absolute freedom from mediocrity. Carpenter's meticulous care in choosing his texts is a case in point. He seemed never to make a mistake in this regard. With even Bainbridge Crist setting *No Limit* (Godfrey Montague Lebhar) and Wintter Watts' *Locations* (Tom Hall), to say nothing of A. Walter Kramer's *The Great Awakening* (Gordon Johnstone), we can appreciate what this means!

# CHAPTER XII

## 1900-1930 (Continued)

### *Alice Barnett, A. Walter Kramer*

A NOTHER song-writer to whom this appeal of nature in her various moods has been only less powerful, and whose reaction toward it has been embodied in many exceedingly attractive songs, is Alice Barnett. It is not for nothing that among her very first published titles (in 1908) appear *Evening* and *At Twilight*, nor that her only song to an original text begins "Hush of twilight, dew on the rose." From 1909 to 1916 there were no published songs, but in the latter year appeared *Serenade* (Clinton Scollard), with which began her real career as a song-composer. In none of her later songs has she surpassed this in delicacy and grace. It is a strictly feminine song, in the best sense of the word, in its shimmering harplike figures, in the smoothness of its harmonization, in the blend of one mellow dissonance into another; and even its one passionate climax is expressed with the reserve of a Debussy rather than the virile abandon of a Richard Strauss. And this is exactly as it should be, to interpret its text. It is in precisely this genre that Miss Barnett has best expressed her own individuality—heroics are not so much in her line. And yet one hesitates to say this, recalling her very successful interpretation of Robert Browning's *In a Gondola*, for Browning was anything but feminine in his poetic style and Miss Barnett has not only been able worthily to interpret these remarkable verses, but to add to them a beauty of her own. Still, it is to this mood of tranquil buoyancy that she turns again and again.

In 1918 appeared three songs, of which *Nightingale Lane* (William Sharp) is the most noteworthy. This is done with the deftest possible touch and is one of her most individual songs. In 1919 she published several songs, among them *Tryst* (Clinton Scollard) and *Mood* (original text), both characterized by the same feminine charm as the *Serenade;* also *The Cool of Night* (Egmont H. Arens), a song of similar style, but somehow with a heavier touch and not showing the spontaneity of its fellows.

In 1919 also appeared Miss Barnett's most important published work, the above-mentioned cycle of eight songs comprising Browning's *In a Gondola.* Here Miss Barnett shows a vigor of style, a feeling for sonority of tone and a richness of scoring, as well as an ability to deal with a dramatic situation quite unsuspected from her earlier songs. Almost the best of the entire cycle is the opening *Serenade,* of splendid sweep and fervor; followed by the *Boat Song,* in which both the gentle motion of the boat and the sardonic humor of Browning's lines are cleverly expressed. *The Moth's Kiss First* is a bit of skilful characterization, while *What are we two* is notable for its broadly sonorous refrain "Scatter the vision forever," and for the admirable suggestion of "The sprite of a star" in the accompaniment, which could scarcely be surpassed in delicacy and finesse (see Ex. 95). While perhaps best of them all in its mood painting is *He muses —drifting. Dip your arm o'er the boatside* and *Tomorrow, if a harpstring, say* interestingly continue the narrative, which reaches its dramatic culmination in *It was ordained to be so, sweet.* It can be questioned whether Miss Barnett was quite able to rise to the sudden dénouement of the stabbing of the lover, though her roughly harmonized and rhythmed whole-tone phrase at the very beginning of the scene is excellent (see Ex. 96). With the entrance of the voice-part her hand is once more sure, and the pathos and tenderness of the text is finely realized. The thematic reminiscences of the opening *Serenade* are as effective

*poco a poco animando*

'gain, what we are?    The   sprite of   a   star,    I

*poco a poco animando*

lure   thee   a - bove   where   the

(96)     It was ordained to be so, Sweet—Barnett

He is surprised and stabbed

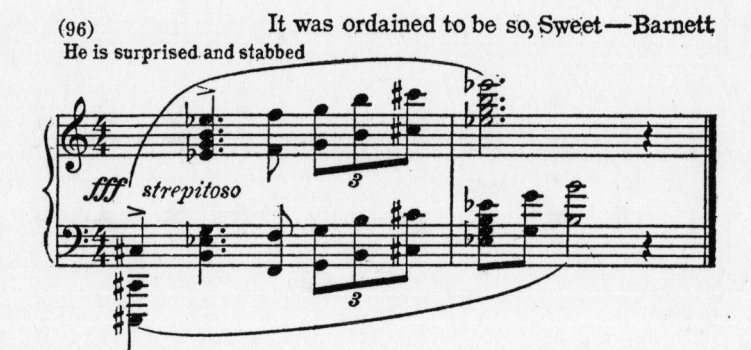

*fff*   *strepitoso*

psychologically as they are musically attractive. I know of few modern song-cycles containing more beautiful music.

Of the *Three Love Songs* published in 1921, *Days that come and go* (John Vance Cheney) shows a particularly rich harmonic background with interestingly managed counterpoint in the piano score. *Two Even-Songs* were issued in the same year —*Mother Moon* (Amelia Burr), a child-song of great attractiveness, and *To-night*, a setting of Sara Teasdale's familiar lines in Miss Barnett's peculiarly fluent style. Among several songs in 1923, *Agamede's Song* is perhaps the most notable by reason of its subtle harmonic scheme.

I think, however, that Miss Barnett has never written anything more imaginative than *Chanson of the Bells of Oseney* (Cale Young Rice), 1924. The skill with which she has individualized each of the bells in turn, Haut-Clere, Doucement, Austyn, John, Gabriel, Marie, is quite beyond praise; and all with true carillon effect. There is no monotony, and yet through the entire song the air of mysticism is carefully preserved. It never falls to earth, but is kept at all times in an atmosphere charged with the clangor of the bells—a remarkably unified and interesting song.

(97)                    Chanson of the Bells of Oseney—Barnett

The bells of O - se - ney,— Haut-clere, Douce-ment, Aus-tyn,

Chant sweet-ly ev-'ry day, And sad - ly, for our sin.

The bells of O - se - nèy,— John, Ga-bri- el, Ma-rie,

Indeed, the entire group of songs published in 1924 is distinctive and quite different in style from all her earlier published work. The texts she has chosen are for the most part exotic in type and hence naturally call for a totally different idiom, and she has shown quite unusual mastery of her new mode of speech.

Unlike so much of this sort of writing, there is nothing forced, nothing which smacks of exaggeration or caricature. Miss Barnett is apparently as much at home here, and speaks with as much sincerity of feeling, as in any of her earlier songs. Probably the most extreme example of this type is *As I came down from Lebanon* (Clinton Scollard). This song lacks the feeling of unity so characteristic of the other songs of this group, but has its interesting moments. *A Caravan from China comes* (Richard Le Gallienne) is attractive throughout, and the feeling of reverence and awe at the words "Her face is from another land" is most impressively realized in the music.

A Caravan from China Comes — Barnett

(98)

Her face is from an - oth- er land, I think she is no mor - tal maid, Her beau-ty, like some

*The Singing Girl of Shan* (F. M.) is engaging in its pure, transparent melody, quite typical of Miss Barnett's ability to write simply, fluently, but with no sign of shallowness. *On a Moonlit River* (again the unknown F. M.) has an ingenious technical motif all its own, which, at the phrase "the gloom is stirred with silver mist of fireflies glowing," makes an effect altogether delightful.

On a Moonlit River —Barnett

gloom Is stirr'd with sil-ver mist of fire - flies

glow ing.

Copyright, 1924, by Composers' Music Corporation

The use of a bit of strict canon in the midst of modern environment greatly enhances the interest of *The Time of Saffron Moons* (F. M.).

*Music, When Soft Voices Die* (Shelley), 1926, shows breadth of line and sustained dignity of style.

There seems no question that without Miss Barnett's gracious femininity, not only would an individual note of very great charm remain unsounded, but our native song would be much the poorer thereby.

It is interesting to note that several of our best known songwriters began writing and publishing early in life. For in-

The Time of Saffron Moons —— Barnett

clos - es." The

time of saf-fron moons,__ Be - lov-ed, comes a - gain.__

Birds in the dusk wak en to

stance, Miss Barnett, after publishing two groups of songs
(seven in all) in 1908-09, allowed eight years to pass with the

issuing of only one song, and that near the end of this period; since which time, however, she has composed and published with approximate regularity. Wintter Watts was very prolific in his earlier years, and in a like period of eight years issued some twenty songs. A. Walter Kramer belongs also to this same group and from the year of his first published songs has seldom allowed a year to pass without new issues. In all these cases the earlier songs are naturally of interest only in what they suggest of that which is to come; and Miss Barnett seems to have chosen the better part when she elected to wait for further publishing until her art had ripened. Among all whom we have so far considered, however, it is John Alden Carpenter who seems to have acted with the greatest wisdom. He published nothing until in his thirties, and the result is that there is scarcely a song in his entire output we would discard. Perhaps it is not quite so direct a case of cause and effect as that, but it would almost seem so. At any rate, in the case of Kramer, as of Watts, there are about a score of songs that we can very comfortably pass over. We said of Watts that his immature songs showed a certain theatricality of effect; with Kramer this immaturity shows itself either in close imitation of the German type of song, with very unoriginal themes and manner of treatment, or a disjointed, diffuse, recitative sort of song with decided French atmosphere. Kramer has always followed impartially these two leadings, and some exceedingly interesting songs have resulted from this two-fold development, more particularly on the French side; while the German song, *Invocation* (*Gebet*), 1922, poem by Otto Julius Bierbaum, is also a truly admirable song. It shows the influence of Richard Strauss at its best, and with the exception of its rather commonplace ending has worked out excellently well. The entrance of the voice-part is managed with the real Straussian skill, and the syncopated opening of the second phrase is of his very spirit;

Invocation — Kramer

(101)

*mp*

Lov - ed Night! On mount and mead-ow
*Lie - be Nacht! auf Berg und Wie - se*

Rest thou, si-lent com-fort-er. On the hem of thy broad pil-low
*Ruhst du, stil-le Trös-ter-in. An dem Sau-me dei-nes Man-tels*

*più rit.*

My de-sires I bring in pray'r.
*Leg' ich all mein Wünsch - en hin.*

*richly*

so also are the artistically handled counter-melodies scattered
throughout the song. In contrast to his earlier songs, these
melodies are individual and attractive—as at "Loved Night,
upon thy bosom," and the brief but lovely imitative effect at the
words "Mother of all piety."

(102)                          Invocation — Kramer

Of an entirely different type, but still showing Teuton influence, is *The Faltering Dusk* (Louis Untermeyer), 1919. Here
Kramer has caught the very spirit of the German folk-song, but
so illumined it with flashes of fancy that not only is it one of his
most sincere songs, but one of the most attractive as well. The
dreamy interlude "like a dance memory" is both psychologically
and musically interesting.

(103)                     The Faltering Dusk — Kramer

Predominantly but not exclusively of German type is *The Crystal Gazer* (John Alan Haughton), 1921. Here Kramer has hit upon a formal scheme of great attractiveness, a modernized and flexible form, suggesting the classical recitative and aria. Kramer's fondness for quasi-recitative effects has often led him into a rambling diffuseness which seems almost formless, but here the close-knit texture of the second section of the song has saved him from this error. Like Watts, Kramer is often far from original in his material, but, also like Watts, he often obtains effects of great beauty; so that in this song, along with certain measures so far from original or in any way distinguished that they sound almost banal, we get such really impressive harmonic progressions as at the words "In other days," and the admirable cadence "Show me of all the one most dear" (see Ex. 104). Kramer's songs show great skill in the development of his accompanying melodies, of which the long melodic line in the piano score throughout the first page of the *G flat* section is a notable example. If we compare this with the similar obbligato in the earlier song, *The Last Hour* (after a poem by Jessie Christian Brown), 1914, we find that while the melodies themselves are perhaps not particularly dissimilar or of unequal value, very great advancement is shown in the setting of the later melody; there is evidence of a far less objective treatment—so much so that the other seems fairly bald in comparison. In the *Two Lieder* (1923) we find the first, *Pleading* (Hermann Hesse), a typical lied in form and style (though a rather ineffective one), but *Unto all Things Voice is Given* (Cäsar Flaischlen) is no lied, either in form or spirit—rather a big concert aria, suggesting full orchestra in every measure. The apostrophe to the sea is excellently handled, but one begins to fear that, if he is not careful, Kramer's evident fondness for imposing effect may lead him into mere bigness without depth.

Before we turn to the songs which show direct and unmistakable French influence, let us note in passing the attractively simple and appropriate setting of Campion's well-known *There is a Garden in Her Face* (1914) and the buoyancy and rhythmic effectiveness with which Kramer has invested Sara Teasdale's equally popular *Joy* (1917)—both of them earlier songs.

The Crystal Gazer—Kramer

Any conscientious accompanist, however, will resent the closing
cadence of the latter song (*Joy*), where he is expected to take a
chord *ffff*, and hold it for two measures with a constant cres-
cendo!   One does not relish being asked to accomplish the impossible.

Of the French songs (as I have called them), perhaps none
is finer than *Swans* (1917), another Sara Teasdale text.   Here
Kramer has made excellent use of his chosen medium: there
is no diffuseness—the weave is close and firm; there is no formlessness—the recurrence of the phrase "We watch the swans,"
with its identical melody, gives a sense of a momentary return
to what has gone before, so essential to any formal success; there
is no harmonic restlessness—the frequent prolonging of a single
harmony through more than one measure giving a sense of rest-
ful poise, attractive in itself and interesting as suggesting the
mood of night with its quiet calm.   Then too, as we should expect, there is the exquisitely molded obbligato at the words
"How still you are—your gaze is on my face."   All in all a well-
nigh perfect song of its type, one in which we feel no desire to
alter a single note anywhere.   How can one pay higher tribute!
(See Ex. 105).

Not so unified, but still more imaginative, is *I have seen
Dawn* (1922).   John Masefield's verses give ample opportunity

for descriptive touches in the music, and the composer has written up to them with great skill.  So deftly is it all done, however, that one is scarcely conscious of the process; we get only the intensified effect of the text, its lights and shadows only deepened thereby, but nothing altered.  Could anything be more delightful than that fleeting suggestion of "the slow old tunes of Spain," or the dainty tripping steps of "the Lady April bringing the daffodils?" while "the soft warm April rain" has inspired one of Kramer's most ingratiating melodic moments,

Swans—Kramer

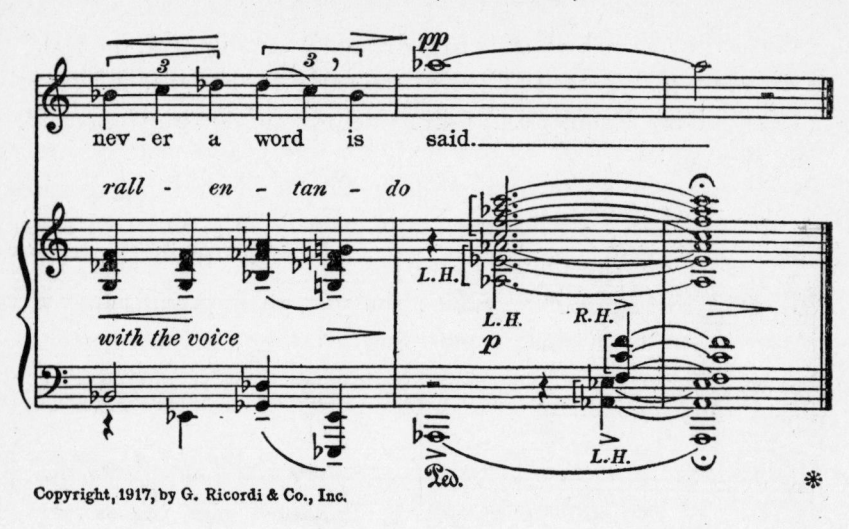

and "the old chant of the sea" is a very breath of salt sea air.
Indeed, this almost programmatic portion of the song serves
once more as a sort of recitative introduction to the main part
of the song, whose breadth of melodic line and sustained harmonic background vividly suggest—as did *The Crystal Gazer*,
above—the old-time aria. Very successfully it is all worked
out, with its reintroduction of the Lady April motif at the end,
except for the fact that this broadly conceived air must be so
unnecessarily interrupted by such fragmentary treatment of the
phrases "and her voice, and her hair." Surely it was not essential that the piano should answer each of these phrases, syllable
for syllable. It is the only structural defect in an otherwise
admirable song (see Ex. 106).

Seemingly only less successful than these two songs, and in
fact strikingly similar in style to *Swans*, is *Now like a Lantern*
(Alice Raphael), 1919. Here is found the same technique, the
same atmosphere. Of shorter, more compact songs of this same
type, there should be mentioned the very sincere and sympathetic
interpretation of Arthur Symons' *Tears* (1917); of *Green* (D.
H. Lawrence), 1916; the two interesting *Sappho Fragments*

(1915) ; the more elaborate and dramatic setting of John Hay's
*The Stirrup Cup* (1916) ; while the early Debussyish *Nocturne*
(1914) shows Kramer's unfailing delight in varying tone-color
and rich euphony.

**I Have Seen Dawn—Kramer**

In the Sonnet Sequence, *Beauty of Earth* (Charles Hanson Towne), 1924, we see Kramer's more recent development at its best.   The free recitative treatment of the voice, which is here adopted throughout the cycle, may be, and very probably is, most appropriate to this particular text; and yet it is perhaps an open question whether the expression of four extended sonnets by such means, no matter how interesting the accompanying score, is not in very certain danger of creating a monotonous effect.   There can be no question, however, that this sequence abounds in individual details of great attractiveness; and in the final sonnet, *Clouds*, the composer has not only shown great skill in establishing an appropriate atmosphere, but at the words "Some clean, white morning I shall thus abide," he has given the voice a melodic phrase of great beauty and impressiveness (see Ex. 107).

*Tracings* (Bernard Raymund), and *The Patriot* (Browning), both 1926, are as far apart as they well could be in their general style—the former thin and cleanly drawn (*tracings* in very truth), the latter dramatic and colorful; the transformation of the very effective processional theme of its introduction into something mournful and pathetic in the further course of the song being its distinguishing feature.

That Kramer is also a sympathetic and skilful arranger of folk-songs is evidenced by his Swedish and Norwegian melodies;

nor must we fail to appreciate his telling example of what a sacred song should be in *This is the Day the Christ was Born* (Frederick H. Martens), 1919. Would that all writers of church music might emulate the dignity and simplicity of this

(107)     Beauty of Earth—Kramer

wharves that touch E - ter - ni - ty,

song.  The *Song without Words* (1921) does not concern us, for
to me, while an interesting piece of work, it is no song in any
sense whatsoever; and just what mental aberration was respon-
sible for the sentimental artificialities of *The Great Awakening*
(Gordon Johnstone), 1921, and *Body and Soul* (Harold Robè),
1922, it is not our province to enquire.

In Kramer then we have seen two distinct lines of development; the one, the earlier established of the two, but continuing
through the years, having to do with the manner and matter of
the typical German song—the same technique and the same content with which Strauss, Brahms, and others have made us so
familiar.  Later came the French influence, latterly coming
more and more to the fore and producing what are probably
his strongest songs.  Here we have seen once more depicted
those serious moods of nature, so loved of Alice Barnett and John
Alden Carpenter, but treated in a somewhat different manner.
Just what may be the ultimate trend of Kramer's writing remains
still to be seen.

# CHAPTER XIII

## 1900-1930 (CONTINUED)

### Bainbridge Crist, Charles Tomlinson Griffes

WITH Bainbridge Crist we find a musical temperament still different from any to which we have so far given our attention. He is primarily attracted to that which is fanciful, unreal. At its best his writing is finely imaginative—a touch of otherworldness is felt throughout much of his work. If ever "the light that never was on sea or land" has seemed to cast its glamour over any song, that song is *Into a Ship Dreaming*. And yet I have always felt a distinct objectivity in his songs. This light of fancy seems never actually to come from within; the song seems bathed in its soft effulgence, but not itself to have irradiated it. Next to his delight in this fancifulness and unreality of mood, comes the joy of painting exotic pictures, where again imagination may have full play. How vivid is this pictorial imagination in Crist's case, may be clearly seen in his cycle *Coloured Stars* and other oriental scenes.

That Crist, however, is not restricted to these shadowy half-lights, nor to exotic moods, we soon learn in songs such as *Girl of the Red Mouth*, which is as spirited and vigorous as any song we know of. But one feels the imaginative mood lurking in the background at all times; it is his own individual and characteristic mood.

It seems quite remarkable that his very first published song, *To Arcady* (C. A. M. Dolson), composed in 1908, should so unmistakably foreshadow this future development. Like Carpenter's first published songs, it shows a sureness of touch not

236

attained so early by the others we have been considering, and points to the future in no uncertain way. Indeed, this early song is quite captivating in its pensive, *sehnsüchtig* expression, and contrary to most early works, is worthy to rank with more mature efforts. It is to be doubted that Crist could even now better the admirably modelled final phrase of the fifth page, "As sweet as grow in Arcady."

To Arcady — Crist

(108)

I found fresh ros-es in my hand_____ As sweet as

grow in Ar-ca-dy!_____

Here was a dissonantal shadow of great attractiveness cast long before!

Of the ten songs published in 1915, *April Rain* (Conrad Aiken), a song of the greatest harmonic fluency and varied tone-color, is likely always to suffer more than it deserves from its very obvious suggestion of Grieg's *With a Water-Lily*. *If there were Dreams to Sell* (Thomas Lovell Beddoes) is one of the striking examples of that fanciful mood which we have spoken of as belonging so particularly to Crist. Technically it has many points of interest—the very effective suggestion of bell ringing ("and the cryer rang the bell"),

the exceedingly subtle harmonization throughout, and the free use of dissonance in the counterpoint, which in connection with the smoothness of the harmony serves to give a certain tang to the taste that is at once delightful and unique.

The year 1916 brings us the beginnings of that happy as-

sociation of Crist's individual temperament with the verses of
Walter de La Mare, which was to prove so stimulating to his
art.   He set no less than eight of de La Mare's poems—slight
poetic fancies for the most part, but ideally fitted to Crist's
style, in their delicacy and refinement.   In *Mistletoe* there is
complete fusion of text and music.   Crist is always skilful in
his declamation; here, however, it is not only an outward fitting of sounds to words, but of spirit to spirit as well.   Most
interesting is his treatment of the repetition of the words "Pale-
green, faery mistletoe" in the second stanza, for their weird
harmonization prepares one for exactly what follows, an effective instance of the added vividness which it is possible to impart to an idea through musical as well as verbal expression.

No foot-steps came, no voice, but on-ly,____

Scarcely less attractive in its whimsical charm and delicacy of touch is *The Little Bird*. *To Columbine* (Kendall Banning) is distinguished for the richness and beauty of its final cadence;

To Columbine — Crist

Dream - - ing, star - ry - eyed and still.____

here we begin to glimpse the tonal glories of such songs as *Coloured Stars*, soon to follow.    In 1917 we find more of the de La Mare texts, and the delightfully droll *Chinese Mother Goose Rhymes*, but it is in the following year that we reach his very zenith of attainment in the etherealized, spiritualized type, in the song that to me is the most perfect song he has ever written, and one of the most perfect songs I know of anywhere, *Into a Ship Dreaming*, this also to a de La Mare text.    This song is the very apotheosis of imaginative fancy, and is of remarkable poetic beauty.

This year of 1918, though not as prolific as some years, shows us much of Crist's very best work.    *You Will Not Come Again* (Dora Sigerson Short) is a powerful song in which Crist interprets a mood quite unusual for him, that of deepest pathos, and he has succeeded admirably in establishing this mood.    Again, in direct antithesis to this, is *O Come Hither* (George Darley), a coloratura song of much buoyancy and oldtime grace; then, still different, the *Girl of the Red Mouth* (Martin MacDermott), fairly bubbling over with good spirits, exuberant, ecstatic, as full of motion as *Into a Ship Dreaming* is of tranquil mysticism.

Girl of the Red Mouth—Crist

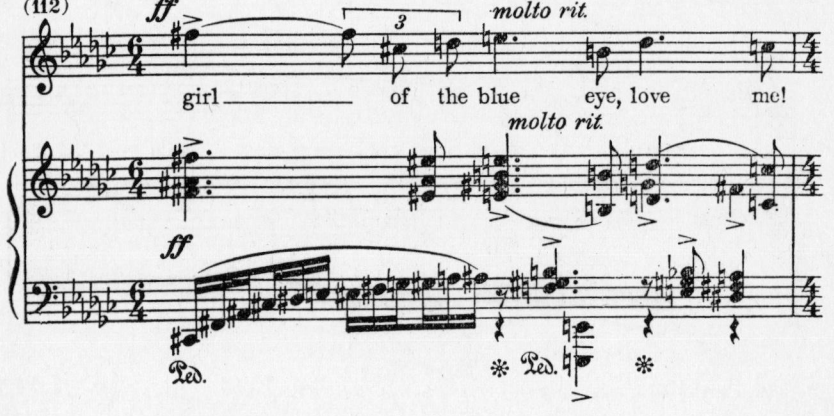

Note the irresistible rhythmic sweep and superb climax at the words "Girl of the blue eye, love me." One can but admire the skilfully managed transition to pathetic appeal at its close. The year 1919 brings us only de La Mare's *The Old Soldier,* in which occurs one of Crist's most suave and lovely melodic passages, beginning with the words "Twas sweet and fresh with buds of May"; the next year appeared *Drolleries from an Oriental Doll's House,* continuing the odd humor of the *Chinese Mother Goose Rhymes,* and two exceedingly poetic settings of texts by Conrad Aiken, *The Dark King's Daughter* and *Enchantment,* songs differing utterly in technique but perhaps equally worth while. In *The Dark King's Daughter* we find an

unusually rich and multicolored piano score, the harmonies un-
loosed and cascaded all over the keyboard with the most lavish
effect, and yet with a delicacy of harmonic feeling entirely befit-
ting the text.   *Enchantment*, on the other hand, is of the closest
texture, but no less rich in its harmonic color scheme.

These lead us naturally to the cycle *Coloured Stars* (Chinese
and Nepalese texts), 1921, in which, as nowhere else, Crist has
given full play to his love of color.   As a cycle it is very successful in its diversity yet unity of feeling, in its skilful dis-
tribution of high lights and shadows; for within its four songs
there is remarkable variety of expression, from the exquisiteness

and restraint of *The Emperor* to the wild passion of *Leila*.   In
the former song there are many clever touches which together
with its simplicity of style make it a very interesting and attractive song.   For sheer beauty, however, the second song,
from which the cycle appropriately takes its name, *Coloured
Stars*, is far and away the best of them all.   If anyone could

better express in music the supreme brilliancy of such colored stars as "Red and purple and green to the zenith, and orange and light violet and lemon and bright rose and crimson all about the sky" we do not know where to find him. Richard Strauss perhaps might do so if he were in one of his inspired moods such as produced *Cäcilie* and others of his best songs, but we can think of no one else. It is a veritable riot of color that Crist has transmuted into one of the most vivid and gorgeous tone pictures that we know of anywhere from any composer. This whole section to the end of the song is worthy of our highest admiration. *The English Girl* seems a puzzle; parts of it are infinitely tender and expressive and the feeling of "foggy brook" and "mist" are splendidly realized, but the song as a whole does not seem on the same high plane as the rest. If in the song *Coloured Stars* Crist has unsurpassed opportunity to display all the brilliant colors on his palette, in *Leila* we get a masterly picture of all that is dark and sinister and poisonous; while its tragic and overwhelming climax, although vastly inferior to that in *Coloured Stars* as far as beauty goes, is even more powerful and dramatic.

Leila—Crist

poi- son flow'rs are  your  vows,   The  dead - ly  fun - gi  your

kiss - es,  The   yel - low  co - bras____ your de - ceits__  Oh!

Lei - - - -

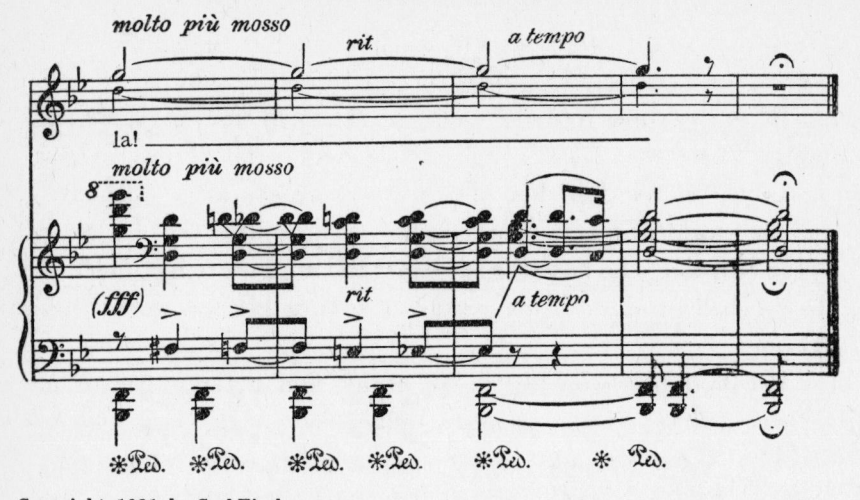

Of Crist's later songs, *Would You Go So Soon* (anonymous text) is a mingling of pathos and power, and *Languor* (once more a Chinese text) is true to its name in its masterly portrayal of the voluptuous languor of the East. Both are of 1923. In 1925 came the whimsical *Queer Yarns* (Walter de La Mare); in 1926, two songs, *A Rose will Fade in a Day* (Dora Sigerson Shorter) and *White Hours Like Snow* (Conrad Aiken), the latter perhaps the best of Crist's later songs. The passage "Can you not change? Run back again to April? Laugh out at me from among young lilac leaves?" shows Crist's skill in declamation, and together with the dramatic climax immediately following, once more discloses his marvellous feeling for color. *Remember* (Christina Rossetti), 1930, is of lesser calibre, but effective.

In the passing of Charles Tomlinson Griffes on April eighth, nineteen-hundred-twenty, American musical art lost one of its most valiant and valued protagonists. There is no question that had he lived out his life, he would have made a contribution to our native music of exceeding value; indeed, it does not seem entirely outside the bounds of reason to suppose that it might have been comparable in our own generation to what MacDowell gave to his. But be that as it may, he has left us much that is sure to live because of its intrinsic worth and beauty.

When we come to make a serious study of his songs, we can but be amazed at their range and variety; and yet we cannot escape the conviction that in our study we are after all merely making explorations in the workshop of his mind; that his songs —the real songs he had it in his heart to sing—were left unsung; the finished product of his genius unfortunately was never to be attained.

We find him working in all styles and making use of all known media. He seems least influenced by Debussy and his school. Whatever may be true of his other forms of composition, we find no single song showing any marked trace of that influence. More clearly he reflects the tendencies of the modern German school, and naturally so, since like most Americans he spent the greater part of his student days in Germany; and when at times he breaks loose from this German influence, it is to the later French and Russian schools that he turns.

The complete list of his songs with dates of publication and also, where possible, of their composition, is as follows:

    I. FIVE GERMAN POEMS FOR A SOLO VOICE WITH PIANO ACCOMPANIMENT (1909). No opus-number
        1. *Auf dem Teich, dem regungslosen* (Lenau)
        2. *Auf geheimem Waldespfade* (Lenau)
        3. *Nacht liegt auf den fremden Wegen* (Heine)
        4. *Der träumende See* (Mosen)
        5. *Wohl lag ich einst in Gram und Schmerz* (Geibel).
    II. SONG FOR A LOW VOICE WITH PIANO ACCOMPANIMENT. No opus-number (1910)
        *Zwei Könige sassen auf Orkadal* (Geibel)
    III. TONE-IMAGES FOR A MEZZO-SOPRANO VOICE WITH PIANO ACCOMPANIMENT. Op. 3 (1912)
        1. *La Fuite de la Lune* (Oscar Wilde)
        2. *Symphony in Yellow* (Oscar Wilde)
        3. *We'll to the Woods and Gather May* (W. E. Henley)
    IV. TWO RONDELS FOR A SOPRANO VOICE WITH PIANO ACCOMPANIMENT. Op. 4 (1913)
        1. *This Book of Hours* (Walter Crane)
        2. *Come Love, across the Sunlit Land* (Clinton Scollard)

V. THREE POEMS FOR VOICE AND PIANO. Op. 9 (1918)
  1. *In a Myrtle Shade* (William Blake).  March, 1916
  2. *Wai Kiki* (Rupert Brooke).  April, 1916
  3. *Phantom* (Arturo Giovannitti).  March, 1916

VI. FIVE POEMS OF ANCIENT CHINA AND JAPAN FOR MEDIUM VOICE AND PIANO.  Op. 10 (1917).  Composed 1916-17.

VII. THREE POEMS BY FIONA MACLEOD IN MUSICAL SETTINGS FOR HIGH VOICE WITH PIANO ACCOMPANIMENT.  Op. 11 (1918)
  1. *The Lament of Ian the Proud* (May, 1918)
  2. *Thy Dark Eyes to Mine* (May, 1918)
  3. *The Rose of the Night* (January, 1918)

VIII. TWO POEMS BY JOHN MASEFIELD, COMPOSED FOR MEDIUM VOICE WITH PIANO ACCOMPANIMENT (1920).  Published posthumously
  1. *An Old Song Resung* (July, 1918)
  2. *Sorrow of Mydath*

With the first five songs (Lenau, Heine, Mosen and Geibel), we find the keenest sort of response to the text, typical German nature poems.    In none of his later and more elaborate songs do we find a more subtle and refined workmanship or a keener appreciation of the mood to be expressed.    They are typical of the style of Brahms and Strauss, whose influence they plainly show. But the wonder lies in the perfection of their art.    To be sure, Griffes in these earlier days had not the varied technique so characteristic of his later work; he repeats certain effects over and over again.    He shares with Strauss the latter's fondness for a $^6_4$ chord climax approached chromatically, for altered chords, enharmonic and chromatic harmonies of all kinds, and a strong, virile use of appoggiaturas and suspensions, all strictly in line with the best German tradition; in point of fact, these songs are as *echt deutsch* as Strauss himself, and, as beautiful and finished examples of this type of song, are worthy of careful and minute study.

The first one, *Auf dem Teich, dem regungslosen*, opens with a typical Brahms subject, entirely worthy of that great master himself.

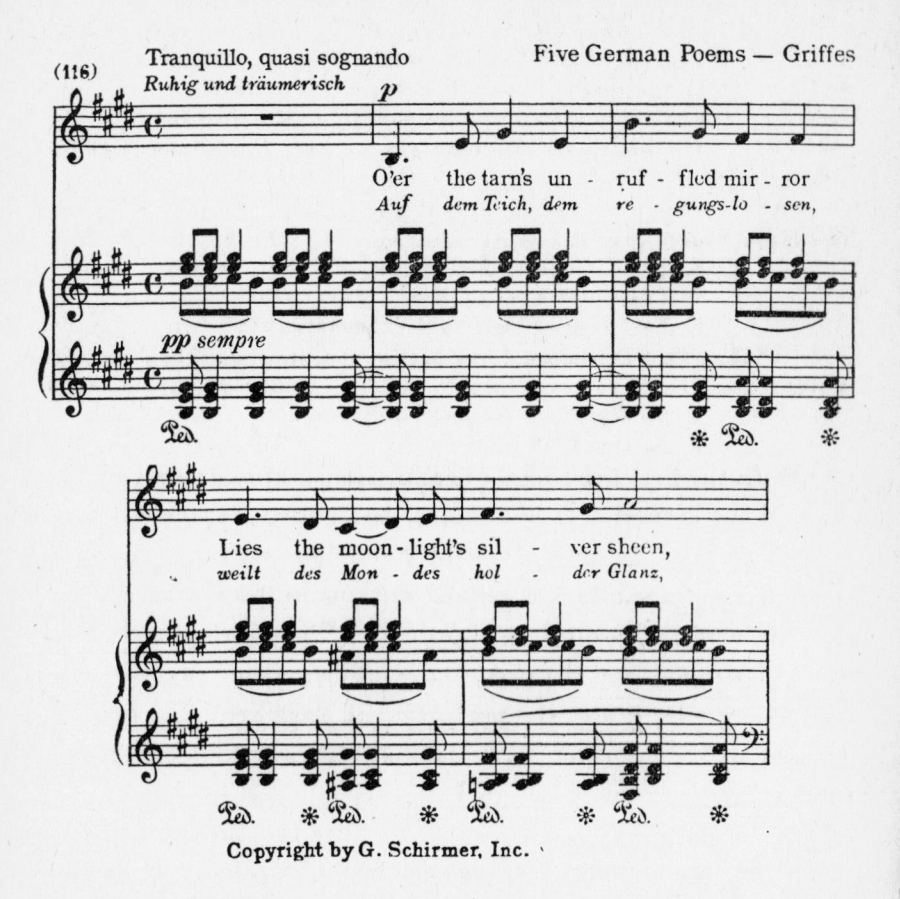

Copyright by G. Schirmer, Inc.

Again on the following page we have a passage equally admirable, but this time as much in the style of Strauss as was the other in that of Brahms. Note the peculiarly Straussian obbligato melody in the piano score. It is this remarkable assimilation of the technique of these masters of song-writing that makes these early songs so notable. Original perhaps they are not, at least in the sense of setting new patterns of beauty; but a rosegarden is perhaps no less beautiful than a garden filled with unfamiliar, exotic bloom, provided always, of course, that the roses be perfect of their kind.

In the second song, *Auf geheimem Waldespfade*, we begin to perceive the shadow of the future thrown across its very first measure, in the tonic chord colored by its sixth. Did Griffes look ahead and see the *Symphony in Yellow* and *In a Myrtle Shade* with their tonic harmonies enhanced not only by the sixth but by the second as well? So early had he been attracted by the beginnings of a new idiom.

The third song, *Nacht liegt auf den fremden Wegen*, shows no continuation of this new manner of speech; in fact, we must wait for *La Fuite de la Lune* and the *Symphony in Yellow*, three years later, for its resumption. Queerly enough, the third and last song of this later group, *We'll to the Woods and Gather May*, shows no trace of this new influence.   Whether the order of the published songs was not that of their composition (he had not yet attained the distinction of seeing the date at the end of each composition, which marks the arrived and accepted composer—this was not to come till some years later), or whether he was deliberately experimenting back and forth, of course we cannot say.   This song abounds in clever bits of technique with a delightful syncopated accompaniment in the manner of Brahms, and again the skilful chromaticism and bits of obbligato melodies à la Strauss.

The fourth song, *Der träumende See,* shows in its middle section a lighter touch than has heretofore appeared—a thin wavy line of arpeggio work, as tenuous as the air we breathe; perhaps a hint of Gallic grace amidst the rich, sonorous Teuton score!

If the prevailing mood of the first four songs of this group seems serious, indeed oftentimes sombre (for the verses of Lenau, Geibel and those of their kind abound in tears and much weeping), the fifth and last, *Wohl lag ich einst in Gram und Schmerz,* is buoyant enough to more than make up for it, and is one of the few songs of real soul happiness that Griffes wrote.   Even here, however, there is an undercurrent of seriousness; it is not so whole-heartedly happy as the later song, *We'll to the Woods and Gather May,* which is joyousness itself, free and unrestrained.   Not so here, for the happiness is too recent, it is in too close juxtaposition with sorrow—"O höchstes Leid, o höchste Lust, wie seid ihr euch so gleich!"   All this is very subtly realized in the music.

Following upon these five songs without opus-number comes still another to a German text (this also without opus-number), *Zwei Könige sassen auf Orkadal,* a ballad, sombre, dramatic in the dark, gloomy way that Griffes loved, nevertheless a true and

simple interpretation of the text.    As I have said before, up to
this point Griffes' songs are of the German type—the workmanship excellent, the spirit refined and often exquisite, with the exquisiteness of *Wie Melodien* and *Traum durch die Dämmerung*.

Beginning with the *Three Tone-Images*, Op. 3 (his first
song opus), however, we find everything changed.    With the
dropping of the German text the German atmosphere has van-
ished.    Not all at once—in *La Fuite de la Lune* there is still
more of Strauss than of anyone else—but with the *Symphony in
Yellow* the change is complete.    Here is neither Brahms nor
Strauss nor yet Griffes himself, as we have hitherto come to know
him.    We might at first think that now we detect the influence
of Debussy, but it has too bitter and acrid a taste—rather Ravel,
perhaps; at any rate, a new spirit has moved in and taken possession.    It is a strange, exotic kind of song, with an atmosphere

Three Tone Images — Griffes

all its own, and beauty, too—a kind of "frigid beauty," to quote a recent phrase. Nor is it lacking in mellower moments as well. What could be more delightful than the unexpected harmonic change at the words "And like a yellow silken scarf," and those delicious fifths at "The thick fog hangs along the quay." Was even here amid these alien surroundings the spirit of Brahms inspiring those parallel thirds between voice and piano?

How strange that close upon the heels of this unexpected departure from all that has gone before, should come the one utterly joyous outburst of all Griffes' singing, the previously mentioned *We'll to the Woods and Gather May*, carefree, utterly oblivious of all responsibility, even of all thought, and that too, written in the simplest, most unsophisticated style imaginable; a song of mocking humor and heedless of all restraint! We may well take note of it, for never again shall we find this mood in his songs.

With the *Two Rondels* of Opus 4, we reach again a new and a still different phase of development, or another experiment, as you will. For *This Book of Hours* Griffes finds in his music the exact counterpart of Walter Crane's verse; there is the same nicety of detail, the same coldness, the same studied simplicity; never were text and music more truly at one. The mediæval touch is cleverly realized through the use of modal harmonization, through formal and delicate counterpoint, the whole having the tint of ivory and old gold.

In the second Rondel, *Come, Love, across the Sunlit Land*, we find something of these same tints; there is, too, the same slight texture, but with an added sense of dainty and graceful movement, again absolutely fitting the text. This, too, is a type which never recurs in Griffes' songs, the nearest approach to it being the one immediately following these, a setting of William Blake's *In a Myrtle Shade*; but in this latter song there is a thicker texture, a more human touch. The same aloofness is here, the same sense of detachment, but not to the same degree; and influenced too, by the very human attributes of weakness and weariness, this subtle change of mood being very successfully reflected in the music. In its use of the most modern technique and yet in its fidelity to the archaic character of the text, it is thoroughly original and admirable; indeed it is one of the most individual of all his songs.

Second in this group (Op. 9) comes *Wai Kiki.* One may well admire the clever suggestion of the native Hawaiian music and the skill with which the piano idiom is maintained throughout (here is no reduction of any orchestral score), and yet be conscious of its frequently unvocal melodic line, and of the uncouth character of much of its harmonization. Still, all this may well be a part of the composer's plan in expressing the psychology of the text. We note the uncanny and sinister beauty of the passage beginning "the dark scents whisper and dim waves creep to me." In this song—perhaps as in no other—we see Griffes' power in painting with elemental colors. The fine sonority of the passage "And new stars burn into the ancient skies":

(119)      *f poco appassionato*          Wai Kiki — Griffes

And new stars burn in - to the an-cient skies,—

and the intense passion of "Two that loved or did not love, and one whose perplexed heart did evil, foolishly" are scarcely surpassed in all his writing.

*Phantom*, the third and last of this group of poems, is a bit of fantasy, attracting while it repels, its atmosphere dark and forbidding, and yet in its final page occurs one of Griffes' most charming phrases, "And hear thee sing again that old, sweet song":

(121)           Phantom — Griffes

and     hear thee sing a - gain That     old, sweet   song, —

Op. 10, *Five Poems of Ancient China and Japan,* we may consider a clever, more or less successful, experiment in the oriental idiom, perhaps more interesting to the experimenter than to anyone else, though this opinion is likely to be challenged by those who, realizing the fascination exerted over Griffes by oriental music and knowing his extraordinary interest in the influence of the idiom of the East upon present-day occidental music, feel that his contributions in this field are of unique and lasting value.

In Op. 11, however, we come to what is probably the fairest flowering of Griffes' art in song, *The Lament of Ian the Proud,*

and *Thy Dark Eyes to Mine*.    In this same opus is included
*The Rose of the Night*, which with *Phantom* and to a lesser
degree *Sorrow of Mydath*, represents the darker and more perverse side of Griffes' art and can perhaps best be considered
another of his unique experiments in depicting unusual emotional moods.    Nowhere in all his songs, however, do we find a
climax more dramatically conceived or more powerfully expressed than in the final pages of *The Rose of the Night*.

*The Lament of Ian the Proud* is sombre enough, it is true,
but presents no unmitigated despair.    Here the composer shows
himself master of his art; there is no hesitancy or uncertainty in
the drawing, no superfluous lines—all is well ordered and sane.
The accompaniment is no true piano score, but suggests the
orchestra with its first syllable; and there is no question that its
effect is greatly enhanced when the orchestra is used; but even
without this added attractiveness the song interests one by
reason of the perfection of its workmanship, the appropriateness
of its thematic material and the reserve with which the entire
mood is presented.    Here is no loud-mouthed ranting, but a
sincere and infinitely pathetic presentment of an old man's un-
assuageable grief.    In this simplicity and nobility of its expression it is perhaps Griffes' finest song.

*Thy Dark Eyes to Mine* is its fit companion, but contrasts
with it in almost every particular.    Where that is pathetic and
a bit austere, this is velvetlike in the richness and smoothness of
its texture.    The whole first section is as sensuous as the heavy
perfume of the lily, but so skilfully has the composer ordered
his effects that there is nothing cloying or oppressive.    Here he
has poured out his gifts with a lavish hand, but always with the
most scrupulous regard for balance and perspective.    Nothing
is overloaded or obscure.    Vital and constantly varying rhythms
are here, a smooth melodic line, rich, colorful harmonies, abun-
dance of attractive obbligato melodies in the piano score, as well

as much attractively modelled contrapuntal passagework for the piano; in short, a song of the greatest charm. The middle section is a bit vague and distinctly inferior to the rest of the song, but where shall we find the composer who never lapses?

There remain but two further songs to be considered, both published since the composer's death—*An Old Song Resung* and *Sorrow of Mydath*. The former is a vigorous sea-song, full of the tang of the sea air and with a powerful climax—as sinister as it is powerful. The *Sorrow of Mydath* is in Griffes' more extreme and less convincing style, though not without characteristic touches of power as well as beauty, the close being admirably handled.

We should choose then as most worthy among the songs we have been discussing *The Lament of Ian the Proud, Thy Dark Eyes to Mine, The Rose of the Night, Wai Kiki,* for their unusually successful delineation of moments of great emotional stress, for their broad sweep of passion, their heroic qualities *per se; In a Myrtle Shade, The Book of Hours,* for the beauty of their detail, their charm of expression, finesse; *Come, Love, across the Sunlit Land, We'll to the Woods and Gather May, Wohl lag ich einst in Gram und Schmerz,* for their finely differentiated moods of joyousness, each one entirely individual and all equally convincing; *La Fuite de la Lune* for its contemplative charm and attractive out-of-doors touches; and *Auf dem Teich, dem Regungslosen, Auf geheimem Waldespfade, Nacht liegt auf den fremden Wegen, Der träumende See,* for their grace of style, their clarity and sincerity both in content and expression.

What then is Griffes' individual contribution to the art of song-writing?

It seems to me to lie in his unfailing sincerity of style, nothing ever done for extraneous effect, everything tending to interpret and elucidate the text; in the skill of his craftsmanship (used in the broadest sense of the word), the originality, appropriateness and inherent value of his thematic material, the beauty and richness of his harmonization, the singableness of his melodies, the vitality and virility of his rhythmic sense.    More specifically we find in his technique one item of superlative charm—his skill (already referred to) in modelling appropriate and effective contrapuntal passagework for the piano.    Here it seems to me he has few equals and no superiors.    Strauss is past-master in this same art, but I know of nothing in his songs that can surpass in effectiveness and sheer beauty two passages of this sort in *Thy Dark Eyes to Mine;* for delicacy and purity of line, for rhythmic charm, for smoothness of finish, the closing measures "afar, a falling star";

for passion, sonority, brilliancy and yet breadth, a dramatic
gesture instinct with all that is heroic and noble, the earlier passage "even of one such kiss, all of the soul of me would leap afar."

(123)        Thy Dark Eyes to Mine — Griffes

These two passages alone would proclaim his distinction as a
writer. We find many such passages, however, as for instance
in the *piu mosso* near the end of *The Lament of Ian the Proud*,
beginning "O blown, whirling leaf":

The Lament of Ian the Proud — Griffes

This is a fine example of maximum of effect with minimum of effort, a situation so often and so deplorably reversed in modern writing.   Also in *The Rose of the Night, Wai Kiki,* and even in the midst of the turmoil of *Phantom* we find momentary glints of this splendor.

To forecast what Griffes might have accomplished in his song-writing had he lived, is manifestly impossible; it is difficult enough to pass final judgment on what he has left us—it is so evidently incomplete.   Indeed, we have no means of knowing even what was his own idea in the matter, whether he actually grew so far away from his earlier style as some of his later songs would imply, or whether they, too, were but a passing phase, an experiment to be in turn followed by something different, or even by a possible reversion to some earlier type.

There are certain fixed or semi-fixed elements throughout his songs which may be of assistance in determining these matters in so far as they may be determined—for instance, Griffes seems to have had almost a classical reverence for form; not at all in terms of binary, ternary and the like, but of symmetry, balance and proportion.   His first songs do not classify themselves readily except as free *durchkomponirte Lieder,* but one is never conscious of any lack of form in the sense of cohesion, of symmetry.   This feeling of unity is obtained in many ways— through persistent accompanimental figures, through recurring melodies and phrases, and most of all perhaps through an almost never failing repetition (modified it may be) at the very end of the song, of some melody or rhythm that has appeared earlier in some important or striking manner.   Thus a perfect sense of unity is secured, and that in the midst of variety—a very happy and flexible formal scheme, allowing the composer the utmost freedom in interpreting his text and yet without any suggestion of formlessness.   Hence it would seem entirely safe to assume that Griffes would never have outgrown his regard for essential form, and no matter how far he might have gone in other directions his work would always have been characterized by symmetry and balance and not left to drift aimlessly along.

In no respect perhaps did Griffes show more marked individuality than in his sensitiveness to rhythmic subtleties. In the three songs of Op. 11, *The Lament of Ian the Proud*, *Thy Dark Eyes to Mine*, and *The Rose of the Night*, with perhaps the second of the posthumous songs, *Sorrow of Mydath*, his command of rhythm reached its climax. In all of these we find the freest kind of rhythmical development. Here is no alternation of different time-signatures, as in his earlier songs (particularly Op. 9); all is unified through one main rhythmic impulse, but this impulse ebbs and flows with indescribable freedom.

There seems no question then that, as far as form and rhythm are concerned, his further development could scarcely have been other than in the direction of an ever increasing wholesome rhythmic vitality, and this tendency would have been constantly guarded from danger of excess through his innate feeling for form and symmetry. What his further development would have been as regards melody and its harmonic background can only be the freest sort of surmise. For, as we have said, his work never seemed settled in these respects; he never seemed decided in his own mind as to what his final trend would be. But it seems only reasonable to suppose that the simplicity of feeling which he showed so attractively in his first five German songs, in the three Tone-Images, in the two Rondels, and not so simply but even more expressively and deeply in *The Lament of Ian the Proud* and *Thy Dark Eyes to Mine*, still further deepened and strengthened by his growing power of self-expression, would have eventuated in songs combining the utmost depth of feeling with real power and vitality of expression.

As time passes and we study these songs more and more with regard to their own development and their relation to other contemporary American songs, the regret continually deepens that this great talent should have been so prematurely cut down. It seems increasingly clear that Griffes had something to give that, so far at least, no one else seems quite to possess. We see in his Op. 11 (Three Poems by Fiona MacLeod), for instance, not only such rich accomplishment—they bear manifold repetition and continued study remarkably well—but still more such sure promise of future achievement, yet richer, yet more worth while, that (as in the similar case of MacDowell) it seems both a national calamity and a national disgrace that such a seemingly unnecessary loss should have been possible. If there are still in our midst those with such talents (or such genius, if you will), overburdened, sacrificed to dull daily routine, may we have the grace to rescue them before it be too late.

As musical affairs are judged by today's standards, none of the group just under discussion, except Griffes, could be classed other than as fairly conservative. He alone had the devoted modernist's love of searching after new truths, even at the cost of the most drastic experimentation. The rest, while making free use, as occasion suggested, of different modern idioms, thus showing no unwillingness to follow where others had led, yet apparently have had no desire to break new paths of their own, or do any intensive exploring on their own account. And there is always this line of cleavage. Human nature seems to be so constituted that there always must be the two types side by side, the one continually experimenting, always enthusiastic, full of the creative instinct, dissatisfied with the present, tired of the old ways and means, looking for something different, rather impatient of those who seem too placidly content with things as they are; the other, reverent toward all that is beautiful in the past, diffident in regard to new means and methods, fearful of losing what has been so laboriously won through the past ages, wishing to see the old types enlarged and beautified rather than new types evolved. And of course this is exceedingly fortunate. Without the one, no progress could ever be made, and without the other there would be no stability of any sort; while without those occupying the happy mean between these two extremes, art would lack its very necessary balance-wheel.

# EPILOGUE

## THE FUTURE

WE have seen art-song in America founded upon the solid rock of German study and tradition, and we cannot be too thankful that this high German ideal of sincerity, of thoroughness, in short "the artistic conscience," was so deeply implanted in our native song at its first beginning, holding sway even to the very present. A permeating influence such as that of Schubert, Schumann, Brahms, and later Wolf and Strauss, could scarcely be surpassed to leaven the lump of our immaturity.

It has been interesting to observe, as the years have passed, how potent has been this initial German impulse through the decades, now and again meeting new influences like the Negro idiom, the Indian element, but brushing them aside and keeping to its steady course till well into the twentieth century, when cross currents have become stronger, and we find many experiments developing along new lines. Much of French, of Russian influence has become apparent. Debussy in his time exercised what was probably the predominant external influence, though where Debussy had his thousands, Brahms and Strauss had still their tens of thousands. Of late these outer influences have grown vastly in power and effectiveness. The advent of such men as Charles M. Loeffler and Ernest Bloch in our midst exerted tremendous pressure toward a modifying of our hitherto strongly intrenched Teutonic ideals. And justly so, for we had developed these ideas and ideals to such an extent that it was time for the introduction of some new ingredient to lighten and

269

brighten what was in danger of becoming a bit stale.  What may come out of all this turmoil of new ideas it is hard to foresee; but it already seems an established fact that in times to come we shall look back upon these earlier decades of the twentieth century as that time when the current of our song began cutting for itself new and deeper channels.

In the general development of art-song in America, as elsewhere, we have seen that its first form was that closely allied to folk-song, with the simplest kind of melody imaginable and the merest chord accompaniment.  At its worst this type of song consists in merely putting any metrical tune to any metrical text, entirely irrespective of any appropriateness in the choosing.  Even at its best we need not look for any close correspondence between words and music.  The most we can hope for is that it shall show a melody which fits the general mood of the text; and when this is the case, its simplicity and naïveté can be most appealing, as witness the well-known melodies of Stephen Foster.

Following this first primitive form, we find that in which the melody and the accompaniment, either or both, begin to become more attractive, more elaborate, by means of contrapuntal touches, richer harmonization, and similar devices, yet with little or no thought of actual interpretation, a general appropriateness of treatment being still the only object sought.  Naturally, it is but a step further to include amidst this increasing elaboration certain interpretative effects, at first purely external, but even so, marking a definite advance.  Soon, however, we begin to note some subjective development—a melody which in itself expresses much of the mood of the poem; a freer, more spontaneous declamation, which, while still retaining an attractive vocal line, is yet able to embody the text as perfectly as does the spoken word; ability to emphasize the turn of a thought in the text by some subtle harmonic change in the music; and an ever-growing and increasingly intimate interrelation between voice and accompaniment, the one constantly enriching and intensifying the other, until we find the texture so closely interwoven that it is scarcely possible to distinguish the different strands, and we begin to realize what fascinating possibilities are thus opened to the sensitive designer of such tonal tapestry.

To my mind this ultimate fusion of text and music can exist in either of the two most distinctive types of song: in that type in which every shade of the text is mirrored in the music—the "panoramic song," as Philip Hale has called it; and also in the other and more general type in which only the prevailing mood of the text is expressed, supplemented at times by such devices as above described. To whichever of these classes it may belong, it is coming to be more and more recognized that modern song can no longer be regarded as merely text plus music or music plus text; it is rather text multiplied by music, music multiplied by text, text so reacting upon music, music so reacting upon text, that the two elements become indissolubly merged into one another, the one really incomplete without the other. In fact, it seems to me that this might well be our test of the modern song: if we derive as much artistic satisfaction from the mere reading of the text itself as in hearing the completed song; or, on the other hand, if substituting an instrument for the voice, thus throwing out the text altogether, we are still conscious of no appreciable loss, then in neither case has the song entirely justified itself; the composer has not risen to the full height of his task.

Consciously or unconsciously, the modern song-writer is following more and more closely in the footsteps of that supreme genius of the nineteenth century—Richard Wagner—and modern song is increasingly inclined to take a leaf out of his notebook; a simple and fragmentary leaf it may be, but yet of his very essence. To be sure, the technique is of our century, not his, but the fundamental idea is the same—that of an elaborated form

of the ancient *arioso*, with its free recitative, at times simplified
until it becomes merely an expressive declamation of the text, at
other times of greater emotional stress, flowering out into real
melody; the entire score serving much as did Wagner's orchestra to emphasize the mood, to italicize certain pictorial or psychological ideas, even at times making use of the *leit-motif* itself.  Or
again it may happen that the voice part merely interweaves itself
with the pattern of the piano score, thus forming a clever lineal
design.  So that not only do we revert to Wagner, but it may
well be that we shall complete a still greater cycle, and perhaps
yet find ourselves back in the instrumental idiom of Haydn's
time, where little thought was given to the appropriate treatment of the text—the mere beauty of the design itself being
considered sufficient.

Just how far this feeling of the varied interrelation of these
two integral elements of song can be carried before song ceases to
be song may well become a point for discussion.  My own feeling in the matter is that much modernistic song-writing has little
to do with song as such, and might better be called by a different name.  True song, it seems to me, must even still concern itself primarily with the vocal line, all else being secondary, though
serving in all possible ways to amplify and interpret the text.
It is conceivable that we are on the verge of producing an entirely
new art-form in which the vocal line as such ceases to exist and
becomes merely one element in evoking a mood or interpreting a
thought, in doing which it may often take a very secondary and
even fragmentary part.  The possibilities of this new art-form
are manifold, and it will be interesting to see its development in
the coming years; but assuredly song, as we have hitherto under-
stood the term, it will cease to be.

And just as in world politics we are coming to see the nations
of the earth in closer and closer association, even their national
policies and very modes of thought more and more merging into

one another, so in the arts, nationalistic schools are beginning to lose their definite boundaries and are coming more and more to blend together until it is now no longer easy to speak definitely of the French school, the German, Italian or Russian schools.  Art is no longer amenable to such definite labels as heretofore; unclassified individualism seems the normal status of today.  So that we need not be unduly anxious over the growth (or lack of growth) of an American school of this, that, or the other, not even of music; but rather place our hopes on the development of such personalities in America and elsewhere, as shall by reason of their own individual genius transcend all schools and nationalistic barriers, and in this way bring honor to their native land.   And if the present rampant individualism, in music as in other arts, in America as in other lands, seems often to lead to extremes and absurdities of all sorts, let us assume that it is only genius in the making—the active process of a fermentation necessary to the ultimate strength and purity of the product, and let us have patience till the time of mellowness and ripening shall come.

When this new art-condition shall have established itself, built upon the four-square foundations securely laid by the great German masters, but modified by Gallic grace, by the wayward charm of the Celt, the Russian pathos and stark realism, the new British, Italian, Spanish influence, and, let us hope, by something from America herself, we shall perhaps begin to realize that art development, like nearly everything else, is rhythmical—it comes in pulses, vibrations, waves, sequences, what you will—and calm is as sure to follow storm in art as in nature; so that after this season of what sometimes seems like nothing but intensive experimentation, we may very likely sooner or later find ourselves in some settled period of art development, comparatively free from all this uncertainty of purpose and extravagance of means so characteristic of our day.

In the meantime it behooves those of us who are but interested onlookers to give our hearty support to every earnest effort toward this end, provided only that the effort be genuinely sincere. For if we believe it to be truly an axiom that art without sincerity is no longer art, then it can scarcely be less true that sincerity in art, no matter what may be its expression, is at all times worthy of one's deep respect.

# INDEX

275

# A Supplement

## to

## Art-Song in America

## 1930-1938

WILLIAM TREAT UPTON

OLIVER DITSON COMPANY

THEODORE PRESSER CO., Distributors, 1712 CHESTNUT ST., PHILADELPHIA

Printed in U. S. A.

# PREFACE

IN MAKING this attempt to bridge the gulf between 1930 and 1938 in the story of the development of art-song in America—an attempt which aims to be suggestive rather than all-inclusive—the author wishes to express his appreciation of the continued courtesy and fine spirit of coöperation on the part of American music publishers, notably: Boosey, Hawkes and Belwin; Cos Cob Press; Carl Fischer, Inc.; J. Fischer and Bro.; Harold Flammer; Galaxy Music Corporation; H. W. Gray; G. Ricordi; G. Schirmer, all of New York. Boston Music Company; Riker, Brown and Wellington; E. C. Schirmer; Arthur P. Schmidt, Boston. Oliver Ditson Company (Theodore Presser Company, Distributors); Elkan-Vogel Company, Philadelphia. New Music, San Francisco.

He also gratefully acknowledges permission to reproduce generous portions of a recent article in the *Musical Quarterly*, together with excerpts from the copyright songs of the Cos Cob Press, H. W. Gray, and New Music.

For the necessary biographical data, he has made frequent reference to Claire Reis' invaluable *Composers in America*.

WILLIAM TREAT UPTON

Pointe au Baril, Ontario
August, 1938

# SUPPLEMENT
## 1930-1938

In the artistic upheaval which followed the World War, the most striking development seems to have been a universal revolt against the spirit of romanticism in all its forms. Hence it came about that the decade immediately following was given over to intensive experimentation, in the feverish determination to find some mode of expression different from that of the past hundred years. In this experimentation music took its full share.

So finely fashioned and so perfectly developed, however, was the art song (for voice and piano) that in America, at least, no change in form was apparent at the time, and only hints of a change in content. But during this past decade more radical innovations have begun to manifest themselves, such as the wordless song, the unaccompanied song, and most commonly of all, the song with other than piano accompaniment—viz., some single instrument, a chamber music ensemble, or even full orchestra. Naturally the added expense of publishing these scores and the increased difficulty of their performance have tended to keep them more or less in the background. The wordless song and the unaccompanied song have also been slow in attaining any distinctive recognition. The result, therefore, is that even during this past decade American song shows *on the surface* little of the changing moods of the world's music. But here, as elsewhere, there are bold and adventurous spirits, and more of their work will undoubtedly appear in due season. It is known that during the past few years some sixty American composers have written for voice with these varying instrumen-

5

tal accompaniments, and there must be many others, as yet undiscovered. Little of this music, however, has yet been published—of unaccompanied or wordless songs, almost none.

When we come to consider in greater detail the technique and content of present day American song writing, we shall find that the non-romantic, impersonal character of atonality, polytonality, and other similar modern modes of expression, have apparently made little appeal to our composers as applied to the writing of songs, although we are not without representation in this difficult field. *Pierrot Lunaire* is not entirely unknown to American composers!

Leaving aside then for the moment the more modernistic phase of American song (whether neo-classic, neo-romantic, atonal, polytonal or whatever) we find that the bulk of our song throughout the past decade has remained essentially romantic. There have been attractive touches of modernist technique, there have been interesting attempts at certain radical methods of procedure, but take him by and large, and the Amercan songwriter, in his heart of hearts, is still what he always has been—frankly conservative. This is not to say that eminently artistic and interesting songs have not resulted from his intelligent assimilation of various types. This, I hope, has been amply shown in preceding pages. We should never allow ourselves to forget that originality is far from being the only (or yet the most important) touchstone in art.

Turning now to the study of individual songs, and beginning where we left off in *Art Song in America*, we note that many of the composers whose songs were there discussed have continued their song writing into this past decade.

Mrs. H. H. A. Beach (1867-   ), the honored dean of contemporary American song writers, shows her accustomed skill in craftsmanship in *Dark Garden* (Leonora Speyer) and *I Shall Be Brave* (Katharine Adams), both of 1932. These songs are interesting primarily because of the fluency and richness of the piano score. More romantically colored is *Fire and Flame* (Anna Addison Moody), 1933.

In 1936 John Alden Carpenter (1876-   ), published *Rest* (Mabel Simpson), *Morning Fair* (Sonnet XX by James Agee); in 1938, *If* (Mabel Livingstone), *Worlds* (Aileen Fisher), *The Pools of Peace* (Joan Campbell). These five songs, composed in 1934-'35, show (in *If* and *Worlds*) Carpenter's continuing devotion to the childlike type of song, which he does so well; also, his ability to evoke a mood (*Rest*), and to write a richly accompanied symphonic song (*Morning Fair*). *The Pools of Peace* is a bit of pure lyricism.

Among the songs of Charles Wakefield Cadman (1881-   ), published during this decade, we find *Like Wind Upon Water* (from the Cycle, *White Enchantment*, text by Nelle Richmond Eberhart), 1930; *Thou'rt Like a Fragrant Flower* (Heine) and *Song of Steel* (Edward Lynn), both published in 1931, although apparently written much earlier—the Heine setting being from the composer's Op. 41, and therefore presumably written sometime during his twenties. In 1936 appeared *Destiny* (Edward Lynn), in 1937 *The Fountain Song* (from *The Garden of Mystery*—text by Nelle Richmond Eberhart, 1915), thus again a much earlier work. It is quite evident from these numerous reprints and the scarcity of new songs from his pen, that of late years Cadman's interests have lain quite outside the field of song.

In *The Way That Lovers Use* (1932) Bainbridge Crist (1883-   ) gives appropriate and graceful setting to Rupert Brooke's whimsical text. But it is in the *Four Songs* (1934) to verses from Conrad Aiken's *Senlin* that Crist gives full sway to his vivid imagination and technical skill. Of these Four Songs, *Evening* is disarming in its apparent simplicity, yet it establishes a definite mood and serves as an admirable introduction to the group as a whole. *By a Silent Shore* carries on and intensifies this mood, and is perhaps the finest of the four songs in its consistent maintenance of that atmosphere of unreality (or perhaps better termed super-reality) which is so peculiarly Crist's own. *Knock on the Door* furnishes needed contrast, and *Noontime* discloses the composer's rich harmonic sense and the extraordinary flexibility and naturalness of his declamation.

*Dawn Shall Over Lethe Break* (Hilaire Belloc) and *The Donkey* (G. K. Chesterton), both 1934, show Richard Hageman (1884-    ) in two well contrasted moods. In the first song the piano score is very full (over full, it would seem), almost unvaried and uninterrupted from beginning to end; the second song is more dramatic in treatment, as befits the text. It has to be admitted, however, that the composer fails to rise to the truly poignant climax of this song. In *The Little Dancers* (Laurence Binyon), 1935, Hageman introduces a humorous bit of realism. *Christmas Eve* (Joyce Kilmer), 1936, is one of those songs delicately balanced between the sacred and the secular, in this case most attractively treated in its first sections, but soon developing that piano etude type of accompaniment which is such a source of danger to many of our song writers. In 1937 appeared *The Rich Man* (Franklin P. Adams), the music as light and frothy as the text. In 1938, *Music I Heard With You* (Conrad Aiken), once more a song whose opening sections are seriously and poetically treated. But soon a broken vocal phrase, an inappropriate bit of passagework for piano, mar what might so easily have been a thoughtful and attractive song. In 1937 there appeared (in addition to the song noted above) a *Song Without Words—a Vocalise for Coloratura Voice.* Here our composer ventures upon a form of song which many modernists feel is to be one of the accepted forms of the art-song of the future. Its freedom from necessary adherence to a given text, hence its greater value as pure music, has been stressed. The distinctive qualities of the voice as an instrument are felt to be best disclosed in this way. Hageman has here written for a coloratura voice, thus indicating in advance the brilliant character of the composition.

In 1930 Frederick Jacobi (1891-   ) published *Circe* and *Aria*, two wordless songs—both of much simpler, more expressive style than Hageman's song. Of similar type was the wordless *Vocalise-Etude* (also 1930) by Blair Fairchild (1877-1933). We recall, too, that in 1921 there appeared a *Song Without Words* by A. Walter Kramer (1890-   ).

As to the coloratura element in Hageman's song, there is precedent for that, too, although it is a type of song little cultivated by our composers. As far back as 1918 we find Bainbridge Crist's attractive treatment of the coloratura style in his song, *O Come Hither* (George Darley), a particularly interesting and authentic example of this type. More recently (1932) appeared Kramer's Aria for Coloratura Soprano and Orchestra, *Parting in Autumn—Meeting in Spring* (John Despard), in which the composer has shown a certain amused and amusing ingenuity in recapturing in the first section the naive sentiment, in the second the objective brilliancy, of the Italian operatic aria of a century ago.

George F. Boyle (1886-   ) and Alice Barnett (1888-   ) are rather sparsely represented during this period—the former with *The Silent Brook* (Emily Dickinson), 1937, which, although not without visible signs of Boyle's very real musicianship, seems somewhat academic in style; Miss Barnett with two songs, 1932, *Nirvana* (John H. Wheelock) and *The Time of Roses* (Thomas Hood). The former seems the more interesting of the two, and is distinguished by a finely developed closing cadence.

The very real danger that lies in a composer's writing his own texts is well exemplified in *Lay My Heart on Marble*, 1936, words and music by Wintter Watts (1886-   ). This song would be admirable if the text were less crude, and the voice part as interesting as the piano score, particularly in its preluding and interluding measures, where we see the composer at his best. As is so often the case with Watts, there are commonplace measures, as well. In *That Little Word No* (again original text), 1938, the music is once more far superior to the text.

From A. Walter Kramer (1890-    ), in addition to the Coloratura Aria already mentioned, we have several excellent songs. In 1930 appeared *Let the Shooting Stars Play Tag* (Priscilla Wadhams) and *The King of China's Daughter* (Edith Sitwell), both simple in content, but of very real distinction. *At the Evening's End* (Sara Teasdale), 1931, is most effective in its final pages, while in *Two Souls* (Paul Wertheimer), 1935, the obbligato melody in the piano score (second page) is particularly noteworthy.

Among all the composers discussed in *Art Song in America*, whose work has been carried over into this last decade, there is no one, it seems to me, who has shown greater advancement in his art than Alexander Steinert (1900-    ). His *Four Lacquer Prints* (Amy Lowell) and *Three Poems* by Shelley, all issued in 1932, are songs of outstanding quality. They are especially interesting in the fact that, while essentially romantic in character, they seem to stand at the very dividing line between the old and the new, the conservative and the radical, and show many of the best qualities of both. Modern in harmony and rhythm, our composer makes use of various details of classic technique; being particularly successful in all forms of imitation, strict and free, in simple and double counterpoint, and especially in the use of a theme in augmentation. This last device he uses again and again—always with the happiest results. The *Lacquer Prints* (*Vicarious, Temple Ceremony, Storm by the Seashore, A Burnt Offering*) are delightful miniatures, generally one page in length, skilfully differentiated in style. *The Three Poems* by Shelley (*The Waning Moon, Ozymandias, To the Nile*) are longer, more elaborated compositions, but with the same excellence as the shorter songs. *Ozymandias* seems to me an extraordinarily successful handling of its own particular type.

Among later works by various composers named on pages 176 to 181, with a few additional names, we list the following:

FRANK LA FORGE (1879-   )
    *Sunset* (Desire E. Carret), 1938
HOMER GRUNN (1880-   )
    *Chant of the Four Hills* (Charles O. Roos), 1937
WARREN STOREY-SMITH (1885-   )
    *Four Songs from In Memoriam* (Tennyson), 1930
WALTER GOLDE (1887-   )
    *A Song of the Sea* (Mary Axelson), 1931
CHARLES REPPER (1889-   )
    *To a Madonna* (Sister Mariella), 1936
HORACE JOHNSON (1893-   )
    *The Rose and the Gardener* (Austin Dobson), 1930
ROBERT BRAINE (1896-   )
    *Promenade* (John Galsworthy), 1934
J. BERTRAM FOX
    *One Lovely Name* (Walter Savage Landor), 1936
GUSTAV KLEMM
    *Sounds* (H. J. Pearl), 1931

Before turning to those of our songwriters who show more of a modernistic trend in their writing, let us note a group of songwriters whose names and works are new to these discussions.

Among the songs appearing in 1930 are two by E. Arthur Janke: *Night Song from Zarathustra* (Friedrich Nietsche) and *Song of Farewell* (Edouard Harancourt), both sincere and musicianly songs; also, *Sleep, Holy Babe* (E. Caswell) by Frances McCollin (1892-   ), one of those songs already referred to as neither quite sacred nor quite secular in expression; here developed with great simplicity and unity of form, yet with effective touches of modernistic color.

In 1931 Kathleen Lockhart Manning, with *Five Fragments* (*Streets, Image, Miss Wing Fu, Silhouette, Voyage*) continues her series of song cycles which already included *Sketches of Paris* (1925), and *Sketches of London* (1929). In 1934 the series is still further continued with *Songs of Egypt* (*Sphinx,*

*Moonrise, Egyptian Love Song, The Camel Rider, Dusk in the Desert*). All these cycles are written to the composer's own texts. As we have already noted, this is a dangerous procedure unless one be a Richard Wagner or a Stephen Foster! Probably of the Five Fragments, *Miss Wing Fu* is the most interesting; from Songs of Egypt, *The Camel Rider*. Also in 1931 appeared *Charm* (Josephine Preston Peabody) and *The Silver Cloud* (Maya Evelyn Boncoeur) by Heinrich Gebhard (1878-   ). The first named song, while frankly romantic in style, discloses the composer's refined and original harmonic sense, the sunny radiance of the text being admirably reflected in the piano score. The second song is a choice bit of musicianly declamation.

This same year is memorable for the fact that at this time there appeared a sacred song whose merits are not to be evaluated solely from the standpoint of its adaptability to a church service, but rather in accordance with the strictest canons of songwriting. In such case the question must and should arise as to how far these two criteria are in accordance with, or in opposition to, each other. There can be no disagreement on the point that the choir loft and the concert platform demand different types of expression, and yet there must be certain common ground between them. It is axiomatic that the sacred song must show no sense of sophistication, no over display of learning on the part of the composer, no superficial brilliancy either for the voice or in the accompanying score. On the other hand, there must be no excess of subjective emotionalism—least of all any trace of weak sentimentality. In the song, *Jesus, Fount of Love* (Eja Mater, fons amoris), by Philip James (1890-   ), the composer has been surprisingly successful in meeting these difficult requirements. The song is devotional in spirit, dignified and sincere. Yet there is ample evidence of thoroughgoing musicianship in its happy combination of modern harmony and traditional thematic treatment—imitation, counterpoint, obbligato melodies, and the like, each in its appropriate place. The one vulnerable point in the song is the instrumental interlude which occurs twice and is far from being conceived in legitimate organ style. If given to piano (the accompaniment is designated as for either instrument) it would still seem out of keeping with the rest of the song. Taken all in all, however, this song is a welcome innovation in the field of American sacred song.

In 1932 we have the thoroughly delightful *Philippe le Bel*, by Wells Hively; also an energetic setting of *God's World* (Edna St. Vincent Millay) by Jacques Wolfe, much surpassed in every respect, however, by his later song, *Prairie Waters by Night* (Carl Sandburg), 1935, which is notable for its rich and varied piano score.

Of symphonic breadth and sweep, with unusual largeness of utterance, is *The End of the Song* (W. P. Kerr), 1933, by Powell Weaver (1890-  ). Published the same year, but quite the opposite in its brevity, with a most ingratiating introductory phrase which is later cleverly introduced into the body of the song, is *Her Dead Lover and a Friend* (G. W. Harrington) by Paul Hastings Allen (1883-  ). Andre Kostelanetz's *Interlude* (George O'Neill), also 1933, is a poetic fragment of real charm.

In 1934 we find another setting of Edna St. Vincent Millay's *God's World*, quite opposite in style to that of Jacques Wolfe, already considered. In this later setting, Sandor Harmati has used the freest sort of recitative throughout—allowing the piano merely to punctuate and give appropriate color to the text. The declamation (all-important in such a procedure) is exceptionally well handled. Also in the same year appeared three *Songs of Faith and Penitance* to texts from Hymns of the Russian Church (*O God of Light, O Jesus, Lord of Mercy Great,* and *Thou Art My Strength*) for soprano with organ accompaniment, by Leo Sowerby (1895-  ). These three songs are epochal in the development of religious song in America. More

"churchly" than James' *Jesus, Fount of Mercy* (already discussed), primarily because of the organ accompaniment, they
are veritable masterpieces in this type of religious expression.
Each is good, but the last named stands out individually by
reason of the value and aptness of the thematic material, the
vigor and spontaneity of the declamation, the rhythmic flexibility of the whole work as shown in its constant succession of
such time signatures as $\frac{4}{4}, \frac{5}{4}, \frac{6}{4}, \frac{8}{4},$ and the richly symphonic character of the organ score.   Were there a Nobel prize for religious
song in America, Sowerby would win it with this song!

*To Anna Burmeister*

## THOU ART MY STRENGTH

Compass:

HYMNS OF THE RUSSIAN CHURCH
TRANS. BY JOHN BROWNLIE, D.D.*

Set to Music by
LEO SOWERBY

*NEW YORK*: THE H.W. GRAY CO., Sole Agents for NOVELLO & CO., LIMITED: *LONDON*

Among the half dozen songs published in 1935 by Vittorio
Giannini (1903-    ), the *Three Poems of the Sea* (Karl Flaster)
are of particular interest. The short *Sea Dream* serves as an
introduction to the more important songs that follow. *Waiting*
is notable for its unusual and exceedingly clever rhythmic interrelation between voice and piano. Underneath these two frequently opposing rhythms, with their unequal phrase lengths,
a definitely patterned triplet figure repeats itself incessantly—
perhaps a subtle suggestion of the surge of the sea. Different
in every detail is the dramatic, symphonically conceived *Song
of the Albatross*, which closes the group. Bold, brilliant, vivid
in its picturization, it seems a well-nigh perfect concert song.
Another song, *Moonlight*, text also by Karl Flaster, is an attractive miniature. Also issued in 1935 is John Laurence Sey-
mour's *The Poet's Prayer* (Ossianic Ode)—a sincerely felt,
attractively colored song.

In 1936 we find three songs—*The Daisies* (James Stephens),
*With Rue My Heart Is Laden* (A. E. Housman), and *Bessie*

*Bobtail* (James Stephens) by Samuel Barber (1910-    ), his Op. 2. Simple in style, with spare, thin texture, these songs abound in telling effects; and in the last named, the climax is at once powerful and poignant. In the same year, *A Valentine* (Elissa Landi) by Abram Chasins (1903-    ), with an individual and interesting piano score.

The years 1936-37 bring us several new names. Henry Sang's two songs, *The Ship* (J. C. Squire), 1936, and *In the Wood of Finvara* (Arthur Symons), 1937, seem strangely uncompromising and severe, but there is a strength, a ruggedness, (particularly in the second song) which makes its own very real appeal. Similarly, Beatrice Posamanick discloses a strong and vigorous personality in *Praise* (Gerald M. Hopkins), 1936, and *Croon for the Christ Child* (Frances Carlin), 1937. The first song is virile, original, and striking—the second, tender and wistful. Both songs show unusual ability. Obviously, here is a new voice worth listening to. With a style much more familiar to our ears, though with less of strength and originality, Elinor Remick Warren gives us several songs in these two years. From those of 1936 we might choose *Wander Shoes* (Helen C. Crew) as most fitting to our present time and taste, in its thin, open score, its rhythmic freshness and spontaneity; from 1937, *Lonely Roads* (John Masefield) for its "tramping" motif at the beginning and end of the song, and its genuinely pathetic closing cadence.

In 1937 we find what is almost our only Tagore setting of this whole decade—Hilda Emery Davis' *Bondage*—a capable and sympathetic setting. In point of fact the year 1937 calls for rather generous recognition on our part: S. L. M. Barlow's (1893-    ) *The Beggar* (from the Chinese) with its vigorous melodic line; Luther Moffitt's *Vine and Eglantine* (Tennyson), extraordinary in its simplicity, but never commonplace; *Vigil*, words and music by Wesley La Violette (1894-    ), with interesting interplay between voice and piano; Theodore Paxson's setting of Heine's *Der Tod, das ist die kühle Nacht*, worthy to rank with the best German lieder; two songs by Max Wald (1889-   ), *The Return* (Richard Le Gallienne), romantic in both form and spirit, and *Beyond the Thames* (James Elroy Flecker), in which the harmonization tends more towards the modernist style, with many of its chords built upon fourths and fifths, yet remains romantic in mood. To this year also belong the *Songs of Three Queens* by Lazare Saminsky (1882-   ): *Anne Bolyn's Dirge, Mary Stuart's Farewell to France* (both to traditional texts), and *Queen Estherka's Laugh* (text by composer)—the first two impressive in their very simplicity, the last more elaborate, more brilliant.

In 1938 appears a song that is unique among all the songs under discussion, in the effervescent buoyancy of its style. With his setting of William Congreve's *See, Sabina Wakes*, H. Merrills Lewis has given us a piano score that glints and glitters with all the cold brilliance of Sabina's eyes themselves. Of more serious content are three songs by Mary Howe (1882-   ). *Ripe Apples* (Leonora Speyer) is notable for the simplicity and directness of its vocal line, set against a rich and sonorous piano part. *Little Elegy* (Elinor Wylie) and *The Little Rose* (Grace Hazard Conklin) are of lesser calibre, although *Little Elegy*, in spite of its brevity, is sensitively conceived, with an atmosphere quite its own. In this same year we have two songs by Randall Thompson (1899-   ), *Velvet Shoes* (Elinor Wylie) and *My Master Hath a Garden* (anon.). The "Quasi una marcia" in the first song proves an interesting motif, but the song as a whole seems somewhat heavy footed. In the second song the composer's apparent fondness for steadily moving rhythms, for Schumannesque metrical divisions, is relieved by graceful interludes and attractive obbligato phrases in the piano score.

As we turn now to those composers whose songs show a more decided modernistic trend, we must retrace our steps for quite a distance—in fact, if we wish to obtain a correct perspective, and approach this phase of our subject from a proper angle, we must go back for a brief moment to the very beginnings of this century.

As early as 1904-'08 we find Charles Loeffler, in 1908-'14 Carl Engel, in 1918-'19, Ernest Bloch, all writing very forward-looking songs. In Loeffler's *Wind Among the Reeds* (1908), in Engel's *Trois Epigrammes* and *Trois Sonnets* (1914), and in Bloch's three *Psalms* (1919), we find works which after twenty years (and Loeffler's even thirty) are far from being outmoded.

It is interesting to parallel these songs with those by Charles T. Griffes, the first American born composer to make outstanding use of modernist idiom. While Loeffler was completing the roster of his songs, Griffes was beginning his song writing with *Five German Poems*, in true Brahmsian and Straussian fashion. While Engel was writing his *Epigrammes* and *Sonnets*, Griffes (notably in *Symphony in Yellow*) was making his first attempts in the newer idioms. Contemporary with Bloch's *Poèmes* and *Psalms* are Griffes' *Three Poems*, Op. 11, unquestionably his finest songs—songs in which he seems, for the time at least, completely to have found himself.

After Griffes' death in 1920, we find two songs by Steinert, 1921-'22; also in 1922, Engel's *Three Poems*; in 1923, Sonneck's *Studies in Song*, Op. 19, and two songs by John Beach; 1924, Marion Bauer's *Four Poems*; 1927, Arthur Shepherd's *Triptych*, Emerson Whithorne's *Grim Troubadour*, George Harris' *Four Tuscan Rispetti*, and Arthur Farwell's *Three Poems*, Op. 43; 1928, two further songs by John Beach; 1929, Farwell's *Two Indian Poems*, Op. 69, and *Three Dickinson Poems*, Op. 73.

All these songs have been already discussed in preceding

pages as setting forth in varying degree and each in its own way some phase of modernist treatment. It is worth while to have these works in mind as we continue in somewhat greater detail our discussion of the more recent examples of various modern trends in American song.

In 1927, the year in which we have already noted the appearance of songs of modern tendency by Shepherd, Whithorne, George Harris and Farwell, there were also issued two widely divergent works as yet not touched upon, by Louis Gruenberg (1884- ) and Bernard Wagenaar (1894- ). *Four Songs*, Op. 24, by Gruenberg—*I Went into the Desert* (Vachel Lindsay), *Larkspur* (James Oppenheim), *Stopping by Woods on a Snowy Evening* (Robert Frost), *The Plaint of a Camel* (Charles Edwin Carryl)—are long, elaborate, symphonically conceived songs: the first fairly epic in scope and dramatic vigor; the second, brilliantly lyric; the third, thoughtful, imaginative; the fourth, appropriately humorous and pseudodramatic. On the other hand, Wagenaar's setting of Arthur Upson's *Song of Agamedes* is pure lyricism, with a most ingratiating piano score, its material interesting in itself and handled with great skill and artistry.

The year 1928 also furnishes contrasting compositions: *The Cry of a Flute*, a simple but effective, fantasy-like composition for voice and flute alone by Quinto Maganini (1897- ), text by Eleanor Norton; and *The Corpse*, words and music by Leo Ornstein (1895- ), for voice and piano. Maganini's composition (subtitled *Prelude in G minor*) is an interesting example of that type of composition so little attempted in America, so frequently found in Europe—a work written for voice with a single accompanying instrument (not piano). We find many such works in England and France—for voice and flute, voice and clarinet, voice and violin, and the like. A recent example is Vaughan Williams' arrangement of Two English Folk-songs for voice and violin alone (1935). Ornstein's song is over-elaborated, very complex as to its piano score, morbid in its text—in all its connotations a thoroughly unpleasant song. Yet one has to admit that the composer has made legitimate use of legitimate means. The greater portion of the song is built upon an ostinato bass of two abrupt and inflexible harmonies, above which, continually repeating itself, moves a more sustained, equally unchanging phrase of four drastically dissonant chords. Again above these there is a varying vertical counterpoint (as it were) of all kinds of fragmentary figures, increasing in intensity as the song progresses, making use, finally, of tone clusters and glissandos. Binding these various elements together, the voice part is fairly simple and at times eloquent. It can be seen that the structural idea underlying the song is sound. One questions, however, whether so much machinery is necessary to project an idea which in itself is essentially simple—further (and more fundamentally), whether such a theme: "In silence he lies upon the black waves, his eyes hidden in the moving waters" is, after all, desirable as the basis of a song.

In absolute contrast to this song is *As It Fell Upon a Day* (Richard Barnefield), 1929, by Aaron Copland (1900-    ), for voice, flute, and clarinet. Abounding in dissonant counterpoint, polytonality, whimsical rhythmic effects, and modernistic ideas of all sorts, it still seems to give authentic interpretation to the quaint seventeenth century text. In its colorful blend of voice, flute and clarinet, it advances a step beyond Maganini's voice and flute, mentioned above.

The year 1930 brings us the truly notable *Five Songs* from James Joyce's "Chamber Music," set by Israel Citkowitz (1909-    ): *Strings in the Earth and Air; When the Shy Star Goes Forth in Heaven; O, It Was Out by Donneycarney; Bid Adieu;* and *My Love Is in a Light Attire.* Taken together these songs show great individuality of treatment, yet all is skilfully ordered, logically developed. Citkowitz, like Copland, delights in imitative effects, and the scores of these five songs are intellectually stimulating, because of the ingenuity and skill so displayed. One constantly discovers instances of such intriguing procedure as setting a theme against itself in augmentation or diminution, and similar contrapuntal devices. This is particularly true of the last song, where it seems as if there were hardly a measure without its hidden imitation of one sort or another. *Bid Adieu*, too, is a veritable contrapuntal tour de force. A long interlude consists of a threefold canon, twice given out. When finally the voice enters, it gives the theme of the canon in augmentation, set against a continuous repetition of its first part in normal note length. After another, shorter interlude, made up of fragments of the canonic theme, the voice enters with the theme of the first section of the song in altered rhythm, set against a somewhat altered form of our familiar canonic theme. All such musical "science" justifies itself only when and if the result is *musically* satisfying. Here it seems to be so justified. Although the third song is not without similar effects, its chief interest lies in the sonority of its piano score. In the second song the keys of *d major* and *d minor* are played off against each other in a bit of skilfully devised bi-tonality. The first song is reserved for later discussion.

In 1932 there appeared *Four Excerpts* from *Job* by A. Lehman Engel (1910-    ): *Introduction, Aria, Interlude, and Double Canon* (voice and accompaniment). Only the *Aria* and *Double Canon* need concern us here. Engel, too, shows himself skilful in adapting old contrapuntal forms to modern usage, but with this important difference that he is apparently quite indifferent to any disturbing cacophony that may result from such procedure when modernistically employed. He seems particularly drawn to the simultaneous use of a theme and its inversion. The first eight measures of the *Aria* are written in this form—most strictly carried out. The *Double Canon* also is skilfully written, but it is a score whose appeal is far more to the eye than to the ear.

In this same year Ruth Crawford (1901-   ) published *Three Songs* for Contralto, Oboe, Piano and Percussion, with Orchestral Ostinato: *Rat Riddles, Prayers of Steel, In Tall Grass*. In these daring songs Miss Crawford has shown excellent craftsmanship and vivid imagination—albeit a somewhat macabre one. Here is no leaning upon classic forms, but a decided and decisive break with all tradition. Whether able to go the whole way with the composer or not, one cannot but admire her courage and skill.

In line with the unusual instrumental combination in Miss Crawford's *Three Songs* is a group of four songs by Vivian Fine (1913-   ), published in 1933: *The Lover in Winter Plaineth for the Spring* (sixteenth century), for voice and viola; *Comfort to a Youth that had Lost his Love* (Robert Herrick), voice, violin and viola; *She Weeps Over Rahoon* and *Tilly* (both by James Joyce), the first for voice and string quartet; the second, for voice, two violins and 'cello. It becomes increasingly evident that at last American song writers are beginning to adopt the procedure of their foreign colleagues, and are making use of other than the formerly invariable piano accompaniment for their songs, thus opening up a field of new and almost limitless possibilities.

As we are to give later and detailed examination to one of these songs, we content ourselves for the present with noting some distinctive effects in the last song, *Tilly*. First of all, the composer, in the first four measures of this song, proves to us once again the accuracy of the equation: $\frac{6}{8}+\frac{9}{8}+\frac{3}{4}+\frac{3}{8}=\frac{6}{8}\times 4$. And this is far more than an interesting mathematical formula, for it testifies to the composer's meticulous care in handling her declamation—an unfailing virtue in Miss Fine's song writing. In this song, too, our composer shows that she is not unmindful of her classic studies, for she introduces a true canon. It has to be admitted, however, that while the voice is, perhaps, the voice of Bach, the hands are indeed the hands of Schoenberg.

At about this same time appeared Loeffler's *Five Irish Fantasies* for voice and orchestra, including a revision of our familiar *Wind Among the Reeds* of 1908. In many ways it is a joy and relief to one's spirit to find such sane and sure orchestration, such wholesome and vital material as appears in these songs.

With *Five Songs* by George Antheil (1900-   ), published in 1934, we return to the customary pianoforte accompaniment. These songs (text "after Adelaide Crapsey") are: *November Night, Triad, Suzanna and the Elders, Fate Defied, The Warning*—all of them short, generally one page each. Although recently published, they were written in 1919-'20, when the composer was just emerging from his 'teens. Perhaps it is to his youth that we owe the violence and desperate intensity of some of these songs—the frequency with which the young composer gives such suggestions in the score as "hard," "defiant," "harshly," "forced," and "strangled." What unguessed horrors may lurk behind the mysterious injunction "strindently" must, at least, as far as the present writer is concerned, be left to the imagination! *November Night* is perhaps the best of these songs, being of particular interest for the economy of means employed. The dissonant character of the harmonization, the attractive pattern, together with its persistent reiteration, provide an unusually unified and effective background. The voice part, too, is of great simplicity. Five different chords in the piano score, five different tones in the voice—this would seem to constitute a record for brevity and conciseness.

In 1935 there was published a collection of ten songs by contemporary American composers—a collection which affords a most illuminating picture of certain phases of our native song writing of the immediate present. It is to be seriously questioned, however, whether a single one of its songs survives the passing of the years. But that is beside the point!

Among the contributors are two familiar names, Copland and Citkowitz. The Copland *Song* (E. E. Cummings), though published much later, really antedates by two years or more his setting of *As It Fell upon a Day*. This *Song* is distinguished for its fine declamation of the text, the voice being supported by a logically developed motif for the piano, repeated in various phrase lengths, much as in Giannini's *Waiting*. The result is a song of unusual directness and simplicity. In *Gentle Lady* (James Joyce), Citkowitz has laid aside all the neo-classic devices of his *Five Songs*, and comes out boldly with a free improvization in modern style. The voice declaims the text in simple but sympathetic manner while a most elaborate Schoenbergian melody for the piano, with characteristic, widely spaced intervals, twines itself about the voice. The closing monotone phrase, "Love is aweary now," is very engagingly treated.

A song by Roger Sessions (1896-   ) is a rare find at any time, and we are fortunate in discovering one here. *On the Beach at Fontana* (James Joyce—how popular this name has become with our present day song writers!), without being extreme in any sense, is a thoroughly modern song in feeling and treatment, rich in imaginative pictorial detail, and bound together by a running sixteenth note counterpoint, which, in its plasticity of outline reminds one of similar passages in the later songs of Griffes. We can vision a singer, already intolerant of sibilants, making desperate struggle with the line, "A senile sea numbers each single slime silvered stone"—but here the blame must lie with Joyce, not Sessions! The disjointed rhythms at the words, "The crazy pier stakes groan," the slipping and sliding and retarded pace at "slime silvered stone" are excellent. The impassioned climaxes, "around us fear" and "unending ache of love," are also notably well done.

## On The Beach At Fontana

JAMES JOYCE                                    ROGER SESSIONS

Virgil Thomson (also 1896-    ) is here represented in a setting of Gertrude Stein's *Susie Asado*. It is quite probable that the

musical setting is worthy of, and appropriate to, the text. I leave that momentous decision entirely to those who admire Gertrude Stein. An utterly different phase of Thomson's song writing will come to our notice a little later.

In *Lilac-Time* (Thomas S. Jones, Jr.) by Alexander Lipsky (1901-   ) we find pure and unadulterated dissonance. Yet, if we grant the legitimacy of atonality, there is much to interest one in this song. Like so many of our younger song writers, Lipsky knows how to handle his declamation with excellent effect, and he understands the art of weaving interesting counterpoint and obbligato melodies into his score—but always of the most drastically dissonant type.

*These, My Ophelia* (Archibald MacLeish) by Theodore Chanler (1902-   ) is a song of quite different aspect, although perhaps equally dissonant. The piano score is built up on a skilfully contrived five chord theme, each chord followed by an after beating octave or fifth in the base. This motif, either in its original or some altered form, is present throughout the song, giving place only once—to a passage of grateful smoothness and suavity. The voice part is fairly continuous, being definitely interrupted only once, and then for but one measure.

The song, *Jimmie's Got a Goil* (E. E. Cummings) by Marc Blitzstein (1905-   ), lighthearted, even frivolous as it is, shows at all points the well-schooled composer. In *The Tide Rises* (Longfellow), Irwin Heilner (1908-   ) gives us an impressionistically colored bit of descriptive writing, done with broad strokes. *Ainsi parfois nos seuils* (from *Scenes d'Anabase*, St. Jean Perse) by Paul Frederic Bowles (1911-   ) opens with a firmly rhythmed marchlike passage, very striking in its bi-tonal character. With the exception of a few lyric measures, the piano score is percussive throughout.

The early song by Charles E. Ives (1874-   ), *Where the Eagle Cannot See* (M. P. Turnbull), composed in 1900, is hardly representative of the work of this composer, who is still as he always has been, the *enfant terrible* of American song. It would be as useless as it would be impossible to single out individual songs of his for any possible analysis here—a chapter, or indeed an entire volume would scarcely do justice to the subject. But the fact remains that whether we agree with him fully, or somewhat, or not at all, we must all admire the pioneering spirit, the sincere purpose, the whimsical humor, underlying all his words and works.

Thus we see in this collection no single song that can be called great, nor even any that can be considered very important. The volume is rather a laboratory note book in which a group of skilled experimenters have recorded certain formulas and procedures which they have discovered in the course of their research. As such, to a serious student of trends and tendencies in contemporary American song, it is invaluable.

Among the more obvious of the new formulas and procedures to be noted in recent American song writing, (many of them of the neo-primitive order) we note the use of the spoken word and and the slide, as in Lehman Engel's *Job*; long passages, almost the entire song in fact, spoken instead of sung, as in Ives' dramatic setting of the Cowboy song, *Charlie Rutlage*; tone clusters and slide, the former used profusely, the latter sparingly, in *Sunset* and *Rest*, texts by Catherine Riegger, music by Henry Cowell (1897-   ). As said before, these are purely objective characteristics. They stand quite apart from the more intimate and subjective phases, the new psychological approach, so definitely to be reckoned with in the study of recent song writing, the world over.

Among American works written under the interesting new formula of voice plus string quartette, there are two, issued during the period under discussion, which may well be considered outstanding—worthy successors in their own decade to Shep-

herd's *Triptych* and Whithorne's *Grim Troubadour* in theirs,
viz., *Stabat Mater* (Max Jacob), 1933, by Virgil Thomson, and
*Dover Beach* (Matthew Arnold), 1936, by Samuel Barber.
Both composers are fortunate in their texts, for both texts are
singularly sincere and expressive. They would be stimulating
to any composer. That both Thomson and Barber appreciated
their good fortune in this respect (let it never be thought that
appropriate texts are always at one's elbow) is evident from
the sympathetic, as well as attractive, scores that have resulted.

Jacob's and Thomson's treatment of the age-old story is eloquent in its simplicity, its reserve, its dignity. The voice part
is always truly vocal, and varied according to the different characters represented. There are certain notable individual fea-
tures in the quartet score, aside from its general effectiveness—
as for instance, the fact that the part of Mary is always accompanied by violin and viola alone—the violin in its lowest regis-
ters. The resulting tone quality is appropriately sombre and
poignant. The part writing is excellent throughout, each of the
four instruments being thoroughly individualized. The viola
perhaps is most eloquent of them all—in itself a truly sympathetic touch.

The score of *Dover Beach* is essentially polyphonic, except
for the passage, "Sophocles long ago heard it," where the declamation of the voice is accompanied by solid chords in the strings.
The thematic material is characteristic, at times subtly descriptive in type, as at the passage, "you hear the grating roar of
pebbles." The composer has shown great skill in the difficult
matter of placing a baritone voice in the midst of a string quartet. The voice never duplicates viola or 'cello, unless for some
special effect. The score is doubly interesting in that one is
conscious at all times that, while the approach is modern, the
means employed are familiar and traditional.

And now, what about the *future* of our American song (or

song in general, for that matter)?  With all the turmoil and confusion existing in the various arts today—in music as well as elsewhere—will song survive?  And if surviving, what will be its form and estate?

With this thought in mind I have tried during the past few years to put myself in touch with as many as possible of our younger representative American composers (including those of the ultra-modern group), for it has seemed reasonable to suppose that if anyone can throw light upon this subject, it ought to be those who, in and through themselves, form the creative element in our modern musical life.  The response has been most generous, interesting, and stimulating.

As our immediate text, let us consider in somewhat more detail than has been possible heretofore the following three songs: *Strings in the Earth and Air*, from *Five Songs for Voice and Piano* (James Joyce) by Israel Citkowitz (1930); *Comfort to a Youth that had lost his Love* (Robert Herrick), by Vivian Fine (1933); and *Toys*, text and music by Carl Ruggles (1920).  Let us take them at their face value only, with no inquiry into source, background, or circumstance, except to note that two of these composers seem to have written these songs when barely out of their teens, the third in his middle thirties.  Thus we remark the fact, relevant or irrelevant as it may be, that these songs represent youth (precocious youth, to be sure) and early (yet ripened) maturity.  In all three cases the technical approach seems sure and confident.

How far, in these songs, can we find answers to our questioning?

Those of us who cannot lightly forswear allegiance to the song form as magnificently developed by a Schumann, a Brahms, a Wolf, or a Fauré, and who yet realize that art is fluid, that while the essence remains the same the form may and must change with the changing years—those of us see in the song by Citkowitz the confirmation of our feeling that song as an art form must and will live—not only live, but live animated by the same spirit that has vitalized it since the days of Schubert.   This we may define as the conviction that song must be vocal, not an aping of any instrumental idiom; that no matter how rich the accompanying score, the voice part must be thoroughly individualized and dominating; that there must be lyricism in the broadest sense of the word—in short, that song must remain song and not deteriorate into some hybrid mixture of opposing types.

Let us now examine the above-mentioned Citkowitz song for the qualities I have contended are clearly to be found there.

## Strings in the Earth and Air

Israel Citkowitz

There's mu - sic    a - long the    ri-ver         For   love wan-ders    there,

We first note the truly vocal character of the music. The voice part consists of a natural and singable melody with no trace of such intervals or rhythms as would suggest instrumental effects. It has its own definite character, goes its own way, deliberate and self-possessed, gives no impression of fragmentariness nor any suggestion of stereotyped patterns. Its rhythms and intervals conform, with a fine regard for unity, to the declamation of the text. The piano score, delicately colored, is never obtrusive, but forms a perfectly adjusted harmonic and rhythmic background for the voice part.

Taken altogether, this would seem a fairly perfect presentment of the mood of the poem, developing consistently and convincingly its primary motive: "Strings in the earth and air make music sweet." The music flows uninterruptedly from the first measure to the last. Any hint of dramatic vigor, of sharpened outline, or of high light and shadow, is for the moment avoided. That this is accomplished without any sense of flaccidity, of inertness, or weakness of fibre, bears eloquent tribute to the discriminating intelligence and the sure musicianship of the composer.

Examined technically, we find the individuality of the song expressed primarily through its freedom of rhythm and its modal coloring. Herein lies its modernity.

The rhythmic ebb and flow is obtained by a persistent use in the piano part of the eighth note as the unvarying rhythmic unit, employed in its single, double and trebled value. A skilful com-

bination of ⁸⁄₈, ⁷⁄₈, and ⁵⁄₈ measures gives a shifting, floating quality to the rhythm of the piano score which, in spite of its modern
atmosphere, is a strictly written bit of three-part counterpoint,
whose delicate texture suggests in its every measure the tenuous,
unearthly quality of muted strings.

Turning now to the song by Vivian Fine, we behold the an-

## Comfort to a Youth that had Lost his Love

Robert Herrick

Vivian Fine

cient mold shattered to fragments, and song emerging as a purely instrumental form.

If we substituted an appropriate wood-wind for the voice part (or even another stringed instrument) there could be no possible loss—there might indeed be a gain. As a piece of purely abstract atonal writing this composition is not without a certain individual attractiveness. But how about it as a song? Where is now our lyricism, our melody?

If we give this song the same scrutiny we gave the Citkowitz song, we shall find that the two works, while apparently quite antithetical in type, nevertheless have more in common than one might suppose. The voice part here, considered as an atonal melody, is well conceived. Indeed its first phrase, from the viewpoint of Schoenbergian atonality, is well nigh perfect, for in its fourteen tones it makes but one repetition and omits no single tone of the duodecuple scale. Rhythmically the ingredients are much the same as those of the Citkowitz song, mingling in similar fashion, measures of $\frac{6}{8}$, $\frac{7}{8}$, $\frac{5}{8}$, and $\frac{3}{8}$; but here the rhythms are vigorous, vital, incisive, while there they were smooth and flowing. The declamation is extraordinarily well handled. Could anything be more natural in its rhythmical nuance than the setting of the first phrase, "What needs complaints, when she a place has with the race of saints?" The rhythmic alertness and spontaneity (almost that of the spoken words) is one of the outstanding excellences of the composition. But as to the intervals—the inflections of the vocal melody—what of them? Is there any possible justification for the falling inflection on the words, "of saints"? Is not this in very fact "treating the voice like a clarinet"? And to what purpose? If the voice part is so instrumentally conceived, why not discard the words altogether, especially since there is very genuine interest just now in the wordless song? It would almost seem as if John Beach might have had this very song in mind when he wrote:

We must expect a new vocal line with unusual intervals and phrasing. The part for the singer and what is commonly called the accompaniment will be more evenly balanced, the voice being treated more and more as an instrument in an ensemble. There are even cases where the voice is effective in chamber and orchestral music for its color alone, where text is of little or no importance and where wordless syllables are used.

Here we have the "new vocal line" and such a nice balance between the vocal and the two instrumental lines that, taken together, the three form a homogeneous whole—a skilful interweaving of equal strands. It is quite likely, indeed, that our composer felt interest in the voice "for its color alone"—giving little heed to the text, except to take care that nothing should do violence to the mood there expressed. One might term the attitude, perhaps, a passive or neutral regard for the mood of the poem.

We note that all the old and accepted laws of melody are cast to the winds—only the rhythmic element maintains a certain continuity with the past. In the voice part, descending major sevenths abound, together with such other characteristic atonal intervals as augmented and diminished fourths, diminished thirds, augmented seconds, etc. The principle of non-repetition of any single tone is extravagantly observed throughout the entire song. The violin part is by far the most sustained of the three and forms the bond tying all the voices together. Something of formal unity is obtained through the employment of free imitative effects, through the striking and frequent use of large and dissonant intervals, and, most of all, through the repetition of the first phrase of the voice part, with slightly varied rhythms, as the closing phrase of the song. The counterpoint is acrid in the extreme, no account whatever being taken of the jarring color combinations resulting from the loosely interwoven strands. The interplay of diverse rhythms is novel and interesting.

Thus we see that as a miniature chamber work, and as a composition representing atonality in one of its peculiarly individual phases, this composition is eminently successful. The question, however, remains: Does it satisfy even our ultra-modern friends as a song?

There remains for brief discussion Carl Ruggles' "Toys." Here we find a texture as purely atonal as that of Vivian Fine, though its construction is entirely different. Our familiar major

# TOYS

Text and Music by
CARL RUGGLES

New York: The H.W. GRAY CO., Sole Selling Agents for NOVELLO & COMPANY Limited. London

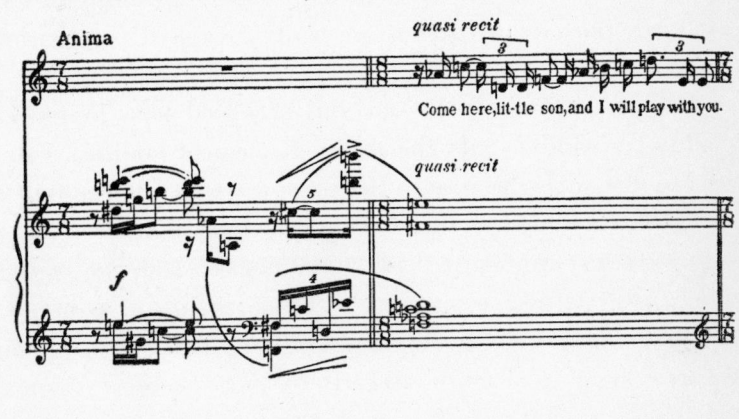

sevenths and minor ninths are present, together with all the other characteristically atonal intervals. However, we find here no formal interweaving of three equal parts—all is free and improvisational in character. In the piano score, our dissonant sevenths and ninths and fourths and thirds are piled upon one another into massive chords, or scattered over the keyboard in delicate harmonic patterns. In the voice part we find the same instrumental feeling with respect to individual intervals as in the Fine song, but Ruggles goes to no such extremes and at all times follows the natural rhythms and inflections of the voice. The rhythmic plasticity in this song is remarkable—more pronounced than in either of the other songs, as witness measures of $\frac{7}{8}, \frac{8}{8}, \frac{9}{8}, \frac{4}{8}, \frac{3}{8}, \frac{5}{8}, \frac{10}{8}$. The voice part, as we have said, is not here on a parity with two other parts, as in the Fine song, nor does it float on the surface of a fluid harmonization, as in the Citkowitz song. It is an independent, individual part, at times accompanied, and at times interrupted, by rich and sonorous music assigned to the piano. Here is no tonal counterpoint or modal atmosphere as with Citkowitz, nor atonal linear counterpoint as with Vivian Fine, but an expansive atonal harmonization, not horizontal but vertical, hence even more poignantly dissonant.

This is then no instrumental chamber work—indeed in its objective aspects it conforms more nearly than did the Fine song to the accepted canons of song writing. But, even so, in its essence is it a true song? Do not its ornate trappings fit illy with the transparent, childlike simplicity of the text?

If, then, these three songs may be said to symbolize or perhaps even embody the whole problem of contemporary song— Citkowitz representing its more conservative aspects, Vivian Fine and Carl Ruggles two phases of its more radical trend— then somewhere within these three songs must lie, latent or already revealed, the germ of Song as we shall see it in the coming years.

Leaving now for the moment these more definite and concrete approaches to our subject, let us look at it in the large, viewing it from various different standpoints.

In the first place, song writing as a *compelling* field of creative endeavor, such as stirred a Schubert, a Schumann, a Brahms, a Wolf, a Strauss, a Fauré, a Chausson, a Duparc, simply does not exist today. I think we will all agree to that, although even here it does not behoove one to generalize too broadly. The song writing of such well known composers as Hindemith, Schoenberg, Castelnuovo-Tedesco, Křenek, and other contemporary composers, is far from negligible, whether regarded qualitatively or quantitatively. But the fact still remains that, as far as our representative composers are concerned, production in the field of song writing is practically at a standstill today as compared with the enormous output of the 19th century. And yet, of all who wrote to me on the subject not one denied the inherent value of the form, and very few admitted a lack of interest in it.

This period of seeming sterility—perhaps more apparent than real—has been no less evident in America than elsewhere, and one of the universally submitted reasons for the condition is the notorious unwillingness of our singers to put themselves to the trouble of becoming acquainted with new songs (particularly those of their own compatriots). The unresponsiveness of singers has been much stressed in the letters received from Marion Bauer, Richard Donovan, Charles Ives, Douglas Moore, Wesley La Violette, and others. There is no question that this complaint is valid.

Quite apart from such obvious difficulties, however, there are some which, while more intangible, more subtle, are no less real.

One of these is the lack of suitable texts. This has been

mentioned by several composers. No one, however, has covered this point as comprehensively as Citkowitz:

Another difficulty is that a composer does not have at his hand a fund of poetry that will permit him to express himself freely in this [the song] form. If we examine any period in which it flowered we shall find that songs were written to texts that belong to the period. There are exceptions to be sure, but in general the sensibility of the composer must find an echo in the poet, and it is usually in a poet of his own time that he finds the most satisfying response. In our day the best poets are exceedingly complex. Only rarely do they attain a real simplicity when thought, emotion, and image are so fused and direct that they become transparent to the composer's musical thought. There are hundreds of poets who turn out pseudo-simple, pseudo-lyrical poems, but these have no reality, and no good composer will try to base his music on them. In a poet like Robert Frost, the thought is as a rule much too complex for setting, but those few poems that are simple and direct are perfect for setting. But the proportion of these poems to the greater majority that are so very complex, illustrates the difficulty the composer has to find suitable texts.

As to his handling a text, after he has found a satisfactory one, Citkowitz adds:

My concern in writing songs is to create a self-sufficient musical form, in which the thought of the poem is fused into the musical form. Adherence to the poem is never at the expense of adherence to the musical form, and *vice versa*. Just as in pure composition the requirements of harmonic thought and contrapuntal thought have to be balanced perfectly, in the same way in a song composition the thought of the poem is a counterpoint, as it were, that has to be adjusted to the musical form.

The value of contemporary texts is stressed also by Randall Thompson, who asks:

Do not the great song periods follow the periods of great lyric poetry? There are relatively few great songs, I dare say, that are settings of text not contemporary or nearly so. A really first rate song period in the United States will emerge when we have a return to lyric poetry or poetry of some other sort that is adaptable to music.

Another interesting point (somewhat allied to the last one) is the need for a careful study of the prosody of a language before attempting serious song writing in that language. Roy Harris:

I do not feel that I can undertake the art of song writing until I have enough leisure to make a special study of the rhythm of prosody. I have considered writing some song studies using only vowels in relation to the mood which the music portrays, but this also involves a study of vowel nuances. . . . Unless one makes such a purposeful study of prosody that one is able to write long natural melodic lines that really synchronize with the rhythm of the words used, song writing is very apt to be a rather weak form of musical expression. This is a great pity because the human voice is undoubtedly the greatest of all instruments and must be preserved in strong music which is created in terms of the medium itself. By this I mean that music is such a noble art that we can not permit it to deteriorate into an accoutrement for scene painting.

This idea is further elaborated by Virgil Thomson:

I credit the excellence of the French and German product to a serious study by composers of the prosodies of the French and German languages. The Italians wrote good songs, too, till they distorted their prosody (for theatrical purposes) into a system that is admirable for sonority, but no longer capable of communicating a text in a straightforward manner. The English and Americans have never attacked the problem seriously. American popular music (evangelic hymns, Negro songs, and modern jazz ditties) is full, however, of interesting and accurate detail. So is the Spanish. Something intelligent and systematic can come out of it eventually, if the musical idiom meanwhile (the popular idiom) can avoid becoming over-sophisticated and unmalleable, as it did in Spain.

Then, too, the whole trend of modern music, in its essential objectivity, its tremendous technical demands, has been anything but favorable to a true song style.

The sensing of an ultimate (or perhaps imminent) revival of an interest in song-writing, however, is expressed by Howard Hanson, Virgil Thomson, and many others.

If this be true, and song is really about to reassert its permanent value as an art-form, among the new and interesting manifestations that we may look for in its new stage are probably: the song without words, the unaccompanied solo-song, and compositions in which the voice is used as merely another instrument in varying chamber music groups, the orchestra, etc.

Frederick Jacobi puts the case well for the wordless song:

The idea of songs without words has interested me for a long while. I realize that in this way one greatly limits the singer's means of expression, but to counteract this I believe there is the advantage to both composer and singer of being able to concentrate on something that is purely musical—not narrative or descriptive: the musical line.

A. Lehman Engel feels that "wordlessness allows formal freedom, wider nuance of vocal coloring; and, most important, it permits the hearer the luxury of grasping the whole structure clearly at a single unprepared hearing. It also gives vocal music the 'internationalism' which instrumental music has always enjoyed."

As to solo-song in its strictest sense (*i.e.* with no accompaniment whatever) Ruth Crawford foresees "a renewed appreciation of the beauty of the unbroken line attainable in unaccompanied solo-singing"—a view apparently shared by Normand Lockwood:

We are living in a Lieder-shadow, as it were, of Strauss, Brahms, *etc.* . . . and I believe that it is well for the composer of my vintage to write his song-with-piano not too seriously and not to dwell upon it too intently—the musical result of his song will be either decadent in the sense of being repetitious, or artificially bizarre at best. He had better and rather look toward a comparatively-long-abandoned form—unaccompanied singing—and write with the fresh vigor and the honest invention that must accompany all processes of true artistic creation.

That the voice will be used more and more in chamber music combinations seems to be universally accepted. Great interest in the development of this particular phase of contemporary song is expressed by Marion Bauer, Carl Bricken, and Lehman Engel. We have already shown by quotation John Beach's appreciation of such combinations. Leo Sowerby shares this interest and foresees larger things along this line:

I can visualize the song (that is, the use of the solo voice with an instrument or instruments) becoming more important from the standpoint of length and musical construction. In fact, I should like to see a Symphony written with a voice part as the solo part, and I hope to do some such thing some day.

In another paragraph he strikes a familiar and responsive chord (to those of us, at least, a part of whose time is given to reviewing various concerts—song recitals among others) when he says:

I detest the ordinary song recital program. There are so many short bits, so many changes of style and mood. Some singers are wise, and give a program of the works of three or four composers, making each group, as it were, a suite. This is much more to my notion. Then when composers will give us works conceived for the voice in which the truly *musical* forms can be worked out more consistently, works which will be longer and more sustained in mood, I for one, shall be pleased. But the poets have got to help us, of course.

These ideas find vigorous echo in the further words of John Beach:

What forms may arise will naturally depend on the developments to be expected in literature itself. Much recent poetry strays far from what we used to consider lyric. But it may be none the less appropriate to musical expression.

There is a new lyricism in literature which music is following apace, and which permits new forms and greater dramatic possibilities. Nothing is more tiresome than an entire evening of short, trivial songs, and, while operatic selections seem to me as a rule out of place in concert, a dramatic form of goodly length can readily find its place in a song recital.

It is quite evident that, with all this rich material our composers have given us—in notes both musical and literary—we have found ample food for thought. Yet we have arrived at no conclusive answer to our fundamental question: what is to be the future of the modern art song? Perhaps, however, we have helped to clear the way towards some answer eventually to be reached.

In conclusion I want to quote in its entirety Lazare Saminsky's sympathetic and comprehensive comment:

The destiny of the song has always passionately interested me, as this is one of my beloved forms of composition. I feel so much the necessity of a musical creator's responsiveness to the eternal lure of the human voice, that I came to consider as a freak, as spiritually and musically deformed, the so-called "instrumental composers," those who never feel the urge of the human voice. To me it seems an impossibility that this eternal source of music should dry out. The newer and vaster forms, like the new opera-ballet and the new choral forms, may absorb the song and deflect the interest of the vocal composer to other channels, those of vast vocal structures. But I am sure that in the long run the song, after having absorbed all the inflections of the new scales, the new colors, coming of late from racial and individual creation, will develop a new song that will express the emotion of future men just as faithfully as Schubert expressed the emotion of his contemporaries. Such extraordinary productions of our time as Schoenberg's *Pierrot Lunaire*, a masterpiece of modern literature, bears witness to my assertion most eloquently.